# Who's in Your Window?
## Sermons that Matter

To Sue—
    Who always knew when to laugh,
and always made me laugh, and
who inspires me on my journey.
        With much love,
            Karl

# Karl Travis

# Parson's Porch Books

www.parsonsporchbooks.com

*Who's in Your Window?*
ISBN: Softcover 978-1-949888-12-6
Copyright © 2018 by

# Who's in Your Window?

# Content

# Introduction

Parson's Porch Books is delighted to present to you this series called *Sermons Matter*.

We believe that many of the best writers are pastors who take the role of preacher seriously. Week in, and week out, they exegete scripture, research material, write and deliver sermons in the context of the life of their particular congregation in their given community.

We further believe that sermons are extensions of Holy Scripture which need to be published beyond the manuscripts which are written for delivery each Sunday. Books serve as a vehicle for the sermon to continue to proclaim the Good News of the Morning to a broader audience.

Dr. Karl Travis gives us a treasure trove of sermons which exemplifies the best of today's preaching. Preachers will benefit from his examples of sermons, and still others will benefit from his insights into the Christian faith.

We celebrate the wonderful occasion of the preaching event in Christian worship when the Pastor speaks, the People listen and the Work of the Church proceeds.

Take, Read, and Heed.

David Russell Tullock, M.Div., D.Min.
Publisher
Parson's Porch Books

10

# Insurance for the Nativity
## Luke 2.1-20

*Christmas Eve sermons are minefields because they inspire thoughts on the incarnation all the while delivered to hurried crowds rushing home for family festivities. Believing as I do, then, that all preaching is local, this sermon seeks its illustrations from events and personalities in a particular congregations.*

People believe that the earth revolves around the sun. It does not. The world revolves around insurance companies.

Early this Fall our children's department began planning an outdoor nativity, with real animals. We realized immediately that we would need a special, one-time insurance rider to keep our kids safe. We our Administrator called our insurance agent and got the conversation. The agent called the underwriter. Then, things got weird. The underwriter was cautious. Careful. He did not think this was a very good idea, this outdoor nativity with live animals, and said so.

What were we to do? Plans were already made. Animals were booked. Publicity was circulating. So, we kept at it. Just two weeks ago our Administrator sent me the breakthrough email. The subject line read, "Finally got insurance for the nativity."

(As we thought, there was a backstory. Turns out, the underwriter covered a nativity once in which a camel bit a kid. We had to promise that we were not using a camel. We opted for the camel-light; a llama.)

Is that not hilarious? Insurance for the nativity.

Imagine a 21st century insurance underwriter asked to cover Joseph and Mary's "situation." Can you see the questionnaire? Can you hear the conversation?

The agent drops by with a clipboard and a Bic pen. Mary and Joseph are both here, hoping for the play-it-safe security of a special policy.

"Joseph and Mary, thanks for having me out. Mary, I see that you are pregnant. Congratulations. Okay, so who carries your health insurance policy? Oh. My. You have no health insurance?

Well, certainly you have received good prenatal care, taken prenatal vitamins. Right? No smoking, I assume. No alcohol. Where did you take your child-birthing classes?

Oh. My. Well, at least you will be delivering your child at home, close to family and to your support network. Sometimes I can attach a rider to a homeowner's policy to cover an at-home delivery. Who has your homeowner's policy?

Oh. My. Bethlehem? You are going to Bethlehem?

Now I do not mean to be presumptuous, but Mary, you seem pretty far along. Who will be transporting you to Bethlehem? Who carries their insurance?

Oh. My. Just the two of you?"

Just imagine that conversation. After all, you know what insurance is. Insurance is managed risk. Insurance is shared responsibility. Insurance is pooling resources so as to hedge our shared bets. No insurance company would write a policy for Joseph and Mary. Young travelers, away from home, with no place to stay. A young mother, delivering a first child. Shepherds, barging in late at night. Wise men, bringing God knows what into the stable. Herod, commanding the slaughter of the innocents. A flight to Egypt. It is enough to give the actuaries a stroke. Too much could go wrong. Too risky.

There would be no insurance at the nativity.

People think that the life and ministry of Jesus were sure things. People assume that God the Father planned every day of Jesus' life, what Jesus would say, and do, and when. People believe that because God is omniscient, all knowing, all Jesus had to do from the moment of his birth was fit the mold, follow the plan, stay the path.

People forget something. It is a big thing, too. Jesus was human. Completely God. Completely human. In his every act, his every decision, Jesus' divine nature and his human nature made their most authentic contributions. And all at the same time.

This is risky business, because people do the damnedest things. Everyone knows that Jesus was exposed to every temptation that we face. The Bible says so. But rarely do we stop to think about his being exposed to the same risks, too. The flu. Hunger. People's cruelty. This was risky business, this incarnation, which makes it so powerful. So meaningful. Jesus faced risk just like you and I do, and he trusted God just like you and I can.

Which is why tonight is so incredibly special.

Some people think of Christianity as a set of intellectual concepts we are asked to accept. So, the thinking goes, learn about omnipotence and omniscience, salvation and grace – learn these words and you are in. Some people think that Christianity is an explanation for the way things work, for how things turn out. Christianity is a cosmology for some, explanation of the cosmos. For others Christianity is about providence, the misunderstood idea that wrongly suggests that everything happens for a reason.

This is the night we get to think through all of that, because on this night, the risk-taking God shows up and with invitation but without an insurance policy. This risk-taking God craves so passionately to be with us that God shows up swaddled and ready for action. Christianity is not first a set of ideas or a comprehensive explanation of the reality. Christianity is a relationship, and that relationship began in that filthy Bethlehem barrio that no self-respecting insurance underwriter would have been caught dead in.

I bet you have heard that song, *From a Distance.* Julie Gold wrote it. Nancy Griffith recorded it, but she was hardly the last. Bette Midler made it really famous. You remember it.

*From a distance the world looks blue and green,*
*And the snowcapped mountains white,*
*From a distance the ocean meets the stream,*
*And the eagle takes to flight,*
*From a distance there is harmony,*
*And it echoes through the land.*

*God is watching us,*
*God is watching us,*
*God is watching us from a distance.*

What a beautiful song. But do you know what? Theologically, set against Christmas Eve, this song is, well, awful. This song is not Christianity! Our risk-taking God is not off in the distance, watching us. Our risk-taking God is right here, in our midst, facing the risks, experiencing the pains, sharing the belly laughs, shaking the hands, breathing the air, bandaging the wounds, calming the distraught, embracing the lonely, lifting the lowly. From a distance, my foot. In Bethlehem, God closes the distance.

There is no insurance policy at the nativity. That is the point of the incarnation. The nativity is all about love. And love is all about relationship. And relationship is about risk.

To say "I love you" is to risk that the other will not say it back. To trust another is to risk that they will not keep your trust. To accept another's love is to risk that you will honor that love only partially, only part way, only some of the time.

And this risk-taking God, the one screeching in Bethlehem, is the ultimate security, the lasting peace, the eternal safety. All consuming, unconditional love, shared risk, and all in a manger.

That is what happens tonight. That is why it is so special, so beautiful. Tonight, God comes to be with us, forever. Which makes all the risk bearable. God is with us. God accepts the risks, with us.

I am a fan of StoryCorps. It plays on National Public Radio every Friday. Americans across the nation go into recording studios and share their significant conversations. The recordings are kept for posterity.

Friday's recording was a father and daughter, recalling Christmas sixteen years ago. [1] The daughter, Kiamichi, was eleven at the time. The dad, Thompson Williams, faced a huge challenge. The family had spent all its money on food. There was nothing left for gifts, for Christmas.

Williams was working with students with special needs, a job he loved, but it was not paying the bills. His wife was selling Christmas ornaments to close the gap, but even together, there just was not enough to go around.

He got a job offer. It would mean more money, but he would have to be gone most of the time. Kiamichi and her old sister, AuNane, would have to adjust. But at least this way, they would have Christmas. If he took the job, Williams said, "I would not be home with my family, and I would not be working with the special-ed kids that I worked with; they would have to do without me. And I had convinced myself that this was the best thing to do because my kids needed Christmas."

He sat down Kiamichi-tet and AuNane to tell them he would accept the new job. "You were real quiet," Thomson tells Kiamichi-

---

[1] StoryCorps, broadcast December 22, 2017,
https://storycorps.org/listen/thompson-williams-and-kiamichi-tet-williams-171222/

tet, "and then AuNane looked at me, and she said, 'Dad, your kids need you more than we need presents.'

Thompson, on Friday's broadcast, reflected on that memory. "That was a time when I was so proud because my kids knew what sacrifice was. I knew that you were going to be good kids. You made me proud."

Presence is the greatest present.
Tonight, God is present with you.
Tonight, God says, we will share the risk.
It is going to be all right.

# Why We Wait

## Luke 2.22-38 and Mark 1.1-8

*Here's an odd confession for a preacher; I am bored with Advent. Its central proclamations – Jesus was promised, Jesus came, Jesus will come again – hardly take four sermons to explore.*

*But the shared meaning connecting all three assertions, that waiting is part of the religious life, is worth an annual consideration.*

You have already deduced from the sermon title that this sermon is about the possibilities of patience, about the rewards of waiting. It is Advent, after all, a season of preparation, a time of getting ready. You have likely assumed what is coming. Every Advent, after all, preachers rail against the rush-rush of the modern world. You have heard the analysis, weathered the critique. Retailers slap up Christmas displays when they take down the Halloween decorations, we decry! Christmas is too commercialized, we carry on, with its parties and shopping and keeping up with the Joneses. What we really need, preachers intone, is to slow down. Smell the roses. Remember the reason for the season. Simplify.

Maybe you think this is where this sermon is heading.

Perhaps we could take the theme – why we wait – somewhere slightly deeper, however. Could there be some unexpected and hopeful Advent corrective to the creeping desire for instant gratification that tempts us all? Perhaps waiting is a spiritual corrective to our collective instinct that we should have all we want, and when we want it, and now. We all witness and experience the contemporary desire for instant gratification. We expect text messages to spur immediate response and phone calls to be returned in minutes not hours. We demand corporate dividends to be high every quarter no matter the need for long term and sustainable growth. Most telling of all, we require that our frazzled relationships be repaired with simple confessions and one-off apologies without doing the deeper work of reconciliation. (Bill O'Reilly and Matt Lauer cannot make things right with a single statement.)

So maybe that is where this sermon is headed – Advent as a corrective to our instinct for instant gratification.

No, we are going deeper still. We are moving right past stop-and-smell-the-roses, blowing right over good-things-come-to-those-who-wait. We are on our way to the heart of the matter.

Why do we wait? Because waiting is good for us. In fact, waiting is God's gift to us. God's people have always waited. It is what we do. It is who we are.

We read two passages this morning. In one, John the Baptist channels his inner Hebrew prophet to prepare the people for the coming of the messiah. The Messiah is in transit. He will baptize with fire. So get ready.

In the second passage, baby Jesus has arrived. Mary and Joseph take him to Jerusalem for the expected rituals. There, old man Simeon praises God that he has lived to see the day.

> *Lord, now you are dismissing your servant in peace, according to your word; for my eyes have seen your salvation, which you have prepared in the presence of all peoples, a light for revelation to the Gentiles, and for glory to your people Israel.*

All his life Simeon has waited. Now, he sees Jesus. He witnesses salvation. He sees the light, the glory of Israel.

That hymn of praise set in Simeon's mouth – "Lord, you are now dismissing your servant" – it has a name. Scholars think that Christians were singing it long before Luke set it to parchment. It is called the Nunc Dimittis. It is grouped with two other early Christian hymns in Luke's first two chapters. The first is Mary's song, the Magnificat. The second is placed in the mouth of Zechariah, John the Baptist's father, called the Benedictus. The Nunc Dimittis finishes the three; *"... you are dismissing your servant in peace, for my eyes have seen your salvation."*

All three of these early hymns echo Luke's larger theme. That theme? God makes promises, and God fulfills those promises. Promise. Fulfillment. God makes promises. God keeps promises. God promised a special messenger who would establish God's reign in justice and peace.

In the early Hebrew Scriptures, the promise for a savior was not about a heavenly emissary who would come someday in the future. It was about some earthly king who was already here. Or kings. David. Solomon. You know the names.

Later, the prophets proclaimed that this special messenger would come someday in the future. That is why many Jews in Jesus' day awaited a messiah to come someday, a messiah who would plant God's flag in Israel's soil and make the world right and just forever. So they waited. Are you jealous of Simeon and Anna? Do you envy the old man, turn green with jealousy that he saw with certainty, that he had of a flesh and blood encounter with the promised son of God?

We are still waiting, of courses. Jesus fulfilled the promises of the law and the prophets. Jesus inaugurated God's kingdom. Because of Jesus, God's kingdom is here, now, but not fully, not completely, not yet. So we are still waiting. That is the advent season, really, boiled down. God promised a Messiah. The Messiah came. The Messiah will come again. Get ready.

Have you watched the news lately? We are still waiting. Sexual accusations. Nuclear saber rattling. Knock-down debates about this tax plan versus that tax plan. Political rancor. Income inequality. Global climate change. Massive immigration shifts as millions of people hope to climb the economic ladder.

God's kingdom? Here? Now? Are you kidding? We are still waiting.

Serious Christians are like kids in the backseat on a very long car trip. Are we there yet? Are we there yet? How much longer?

We are waiting. We are waiting for decency to prevail. We are waiting for peace to break out. We are waiting for justice to roll down like the waters. We are waiting for kindness, compassion, and creativity to overwhelm cruelty, heartlessness, and boredom. We are waiting.

Do you know why we wait? Do you realize why God leaves us waiting?

I read recently that an unholy race has emerged among American college students. In 2008, the majority of students who sought counseling named depression their number one emotional challenge. The next year, in 2009, the majority cited anxiety. [2] Every year since, anxiety has stretched its lead over depression as the

---

[2] https://www.insidehighered.com/news/2017/03/29/anxiety-and-depression-are-primary-concerns-students-seeking-counseling-services.

number one emotional threat experienced by American college students.

If that is not enough to snatch your attention, catch this; in the last decade, the number of suicidal kids admitted to children's hospitals has doubled. [3] College students and teenagers amplify what our world is coming to, and their prophecy is powerful. Anxiety about the future is overshadowing sadness about the past.

If depression is clinging to yesterday and anxiety is rushing to tomorrow, waiting is anxiety's antidote.

Waiting calms the narcissistic nerves. Waiting lowers the self-elevating blood pressure. Waiting redirects our gaze from the mirror to the mystery of God. Because God's reign is not first about us, about what we want, about our vision for the world. We have roles, you and I, in an ongoing drama, a living drama, on an eternal stage. Ours are important parts, significant roles. We each get plenty of lines, lots to say, loads of action. But our roles are supporting roles.

This storyline is bigger and older and more compelling than we have imagined, than we can ever imagine. It includes us, all right, but it does not include only us. It is not about us, not first about us, anyway. It is about God. It is God's story, God's drama. God is the playwright and God has written a part for each of us.

As playwrights go, God has a penchant for long stories. God's story is a very long story. So we wait. We wait every day. Like our ancestors. Sarah and Abraham waited for that baby, that baby boy who would carry their people into the future. The Hebrews waited for release from Egyptian bondage. The exiles waited to return home. The prophets waited for God's people to follow God's word. Then, the disciples waited, waited on Good Friday to see what God would do on Easter Sunday. The apostles waited for God's Spirit to form the church. Early Christians waited for freedom from Roman treachery, from Pagan idolatry. Early Protestants waited for the church's reform, even if it meant crossing oceans and starting over.

We wait. That is what people do when role playing in God's eternal drama. Our entire lives are joyous, exultant, patient efforts to play our roles in the everlasting story of God.

Maybe you have noticed that we post recordings of sermons on our congregation's website. From time to time I ask about sermon

---

[3] http://www.aappublications.org/news/2017/05/04/PASSuicide050417.

statistics – which sermons are the most listened to, the most downloaded. These stats help me gauge which themes and topics are finding the greatest audience. Far and away the most listened to and downloaded sermon I have preached is a sermon on letting go of expectations. In that sermon I suggested that expectations are folly. They are our limited projections upon the future. The problem with expectations, then, is that our personal anticipations of what we think should be blind us to the possibility of what might be. Consumed with what we want to happen, we close ourselves to what God might do.

Anxiety is the product of so wanting the future to unfold in a certain way that we worry in advance that it will not.

Waiting is anxiety's antidote. Waiting is God's gift. Learning to wait is learning to trust. Learning to trust is learning to live.

And that is why we wait.

# What Then Should We Do?

## Luke 3.7-18

*This sermon was preached on the third Sunday of Advent 2012, as the congregation baptized several children, just a week after a gunman killed 26 people – 20 of them children – at Sandy Hook Elementary School.*

Sometimes, just before the Prayer of Confession, our liturgists say, "God loves you just the way you are, and God loves you too much to let you stay this way." In our pleasant, gentle, non-confrontational 21st century way, we use those assuring words as a Call to Confession. I see this saying everywhere these days. Some people put these words on their refrigerators. I suppose they serve well there, particularly if overeating is overwhelming a person's sense of lovability. It might be nice to remember, when going for the second bowl of ice cream, that "God loves you just way you are." Reaching for the Blue Bell might be a tad more difficult against the second part, however; "God loves you too much to let you stay this way." The second part of the sentence seems not so much a Call to Confession as a call to repentance.

You know what repentance is. Repentance is a choice to change. Repentance is a decision for transformation. Repentance is a deliberate U-turn, a resolution of will to walk away – to walk away from the refrigerator, or from the bottle, or to walk away from greed or covetousness or to walk away from the most destructive sin of all: the illusion that we can live without God, that we can be whole and holy on our own.

Jesus was the Messiah. People kept walking away from God, so God walked toward people.

John the Baptist came to announce Jesus' arrival. Last Sunday we remembered how John the Baptist "went into all the region around the Jordan, proclaiming a baptism of repentance for the forgiveness of sins." Baptism was connected to repentance. People repented, then they were baptized.

In today's Gospel reading, the crowds are coming. John is preaching and baptizing. Sometimes preachers begin sermons with a funny story, maybe even a joke. John did not. John did not gently survey the crowd and announce, "God loves you just the way you are." John looked the crowd over, took a deep breath, and bellowed,

> *"Brood of snakes! What do you think you are doing slithering down here to the river? Do you think a little water on your snakeskins is going to deflect God's judgment? It is your life that must change, not your skin."* [4]

Which better motivates you, "God loves you just the way you are," or, "You brood of vipers"? Both are calls to repentance. Which do you prefer? If God calls you to change, do you want to begin with accusation, or with affirmation?

Truth told, both can work. It depends on the audience, and it depends the speaker. Either way, the goal is the same: change. The world needs to change. And that includes us. We need to change.

I am probably not alone in resenting the annual intrusion of John the Baptist. I mean, amidst the annual joys of Advent wreaths and mistletoe, right in the middle of manger scenes and holiday parties, John rushes in calling us a bunch of snakes. If this is religion, who needs it? Who needs name-calling, fire-breathing, hellfire-and-brimstone religion? We prefer our religion warm, not hot, with two lumps of sugar. You catch more flies with sugar, after all.

So John seems out of season, in Advent and in the 21st century. I am just sayin' …

But this morning, today, right now, John seems right on time, for at least two reasons.

First, John baptized people and this morning we do the same. John baptized on the way to preparing people for the coming of the Prince of Peace. That is Advent. We do the same. Somehow this baptismal ritual races across time and connects the River Jordan to the Trinity River. John's work is still holy and important. The waters of baptism continue to get us ready for Jesus.

Here is a second reason John seems welcome on this day. When John calls his audience a bunch of snakes, he was talking to everyone. He was preaching to "the crowd." Luke says that "the crowds" came to be baptized. Otherwise in the Gospels, when John or Jesus either one call people snakes or "wicked" or "perverse," they are talking to specific people. They are talking to Pharisees or to Sadducees, to

---

[4] Luke 3:7-8, *The Message*, Eugene Peterson.

religious leaders or to individuals, Zacchaeus maybe, or the woman at the well.

Today John speaks to "the crowd." John calls the entire crowd to repentance by calling them snakes, which does not so much mean that everyone in the crowd is a snake so much as it means that they were all in the mess together. And today, with the news from Sandy Hook, we are strikingly aware of being in this together. Life is shared. What happens to you, shapes me, and what happens to me, shapes you, and as the world goes flat and stories go viral and our interconnectedness becomes all the more obvious. We are in this together.

Which is a beautiful promise today. As personal as baptism is, it is never private. Sure, today we announce and celebrate that God knows by name each and every child touched by these waters. Yet baptism also signifies their welcome into the family of God, grafts them into God's crowd. Truth told, given that awful things can happen even to children, we are in this together. We are interconnected.

That crowd heard John's bellowing and name-calling and truth telling and felt about as hopeless as you might be feeling today. The world can seem a dark and heavy place, full of snakes.

Do you remember what they asked John? They asked a direct question, a pointed question, a powerful question. They asked John, "What then should we do?" They did not ask, "What should I do?" The crowd wondered about ethics, about community action. They asked John about the ethics of community life.

John was quick with the answer. To tax collectors, John said, "do not steal." To soldiers, John said, "do not extort." To everyone, John said, "share." If someone needs a coat and you have two, offer the second.

In other words, the Messiah is not coming to solve all of our problems. The Messiah inspires us to confront our problems together with God's help.

Maybe you saw the story about that New York City cop who spontaneously bought a homeless man a pair of boots on a cold night. Some tourist took a picture of it and posted it on the internet. The picture went viral. I know, I know, the story got more complicated when the homeless man hid the boots for fear of being robbed of them. I know about the homeless man's brother, who said that he was always welcome in their home but that he had chosen to remain homeless. I know. [5]

But nothing changes the fact that a New York City cop reached into his pocket to help a barefooted man on a cold night.

And maybe you saw the story of Warren Buffet's son, an honest-to-goodness dirt farmer, who has dedicated himself to solving the problem of hunger. [6]

This crowd we belong to, this slithering mass, might seem to you obscured by Connecticut shadows. But for every such headline there are others, too, other evidences that countless people have heard John's sermon about doing right and sharing all and changing the world. The Bible never says that darkness will disappear. God promises rather that the light has come, and that darkness will never put it out.

Which is why John is welcome this year, today. The only possible way to move the world towards what it should be is to confront the world as it actually is.

Great news! Advent and Christmas are about so much more than tranquil scenes, shining stars, gentle shepherds, and singing angels. Jesus arrives in the dark. He shines with a vision of how things are yet to be. And you, God thinks so much of you, and this morning thinks so much of these children, that God reaches down and scoops us into God's crowd. God calls us to participate in the ethics of waiting.

The world needs to change. So do we.

God loves us just as we are. And God refuses to let us stay this way.

---

[5] "Homeless man given boots by cop is seen shoeless," NY DailyNews.com, December 3, 2012.
[6] "The Good Farmer: One Man's crusade to stamp out hunger in America," *Parade*, December 2, 2012.

# Look Who's Talking

## Luke 3.15-17, 21-22

*This sermon on the baptism of Jesus, preached in a presidential election year, happened also to coincide with the ordination of elders.*

What would you have heard if you had been there? If you had been there the day John baptized Jesus, what would you have heard?

Luke says that Jesus was baptized "when all the people were baptized" so we know that there were others. A crowd, even. Jesus was not even the first to be baptized. Apparently, he stood in line, waited his turn. Then John baptized him. After, "the Holy Spirit descended upon him" and a voice came from heaven. "You are my Son, the Beloved, with you I am well pleased."

Would you have heard that voice, speaking to Jesus? "You are my son, the Beloved." If you heard it, you would have been eavesdropping. Clearly, the Father was conversing with Jesus. "You are my son." The Father spoke personally to the Son. It is up for grabs whether Jesus was the only person who heard the voice, or if everyone within earshot heard the Father's voice. Matthew tells the story differently.

In Luke, the voice says, "You are my son." In Matthew, the voice says, "This is my son, the beloved."

In Luke, the Father intends for the Son to understand his identity. In Matthew, the voice intends for the crowd to understand Jesus' identity.

In Luke, Jesus is affirmed. In Matthew, Jesus is given authority so that the crowd will follow him.

This is a very important difference. It gets to the core of what it means to lead, and what it means to trust those who lead us. That is worth thinking about this morning, as we ordain those we believe God has called to lead us.

We do so at the beginning of a Presidential election cycle. Well, wait – I should say that we are in the middle of a presidential election cycle. Though no state has yet to hold an election primary, candidates have already been campaigning for over a year. They spend hundreds of millions of dollars begging our attention. Every interview, each stump speech, every television commercial is designed to say, "Look at me. Vote for me. I am the one to lead us, and, if you are smart, you will agree with me."

When I was a teenager I ran for office in some organization or other and my parents got me a very special baseball cap. It had two bills, sewn at a right angle to the other. The cap read, "Which way did they do? I am their leader." Presidential campaigns feel like that. A dozen or so candidates arrive in rented busses wearing those hats. They yell and bicker, attack and defend. After a few months it is down to two, then to one, then we cast our votes and watch the inaugural. Next, in only two more years, we start all over. This is not even to mention the races for Congress, or the state legislature, or every office down the ballot. Such is life in a democracy, candidates yelling for our attention. "Look at me. Vote for me. I want the authority to lead you."

In the middle of this election haze a few dazed disciples have been preparing for the coming moment when they will kneel and answer the church's constitutional questions and make their promises to lead our congregation. What is more, they will promise not only to lead us for the coming three years. They will promise to follow Jesus in a new way, in a deeper way than they ever have before. They will promise for the rest of their lives to work for nothing short of the transformation of the world.

If that is not crazy enough, here is the really audacious part; they did not ask to do it. They did not decide to run for elder. None of them had forethought. They never once put on a crazy cap and said, "Look at me." Instead, representatives from the congregation appeared at their doorsteps and asked if God might be calling them into ordained life. At that moment, nearly all of them – maybe all of them – heard their own inner voice. I have been doing this for almost twenty-five years and almost without exception people tell me that when the Nominating Committee arrives, and they suddenly hear their inner voice, their inner voice says the same thing: Are you kidding? Me?

But after the inner voice's initial reaction, the person pauses, and prays, and thinks some more. It is then that another voice speaks, a deeper voice, and it speaks over and often against the individual's inner voice. This new voice says, "Yes. You. Do not be afraid. We will do it together."

So the person phones the Nominating Committee and agrees to do it, surprised as she may be. Then the congregation meets and elects the candidates. Then training begins. If you did not know it, these elders-to-be have spent a good part of the autumn learning some good portion of what they will need to know to lead well. And somewhere along the way these elders-to-be generally hear this deeper voice whisper something else. After it says, "Do not be afraid. We will do it together," the voice adds, "You are my child."

This matter, too. It matters because people who have heard the affirmation of this deeper voice are much less likely to say, "Look at me" and much more likely to say, "Look at God."

That is what happened with Jesus. He said that only his father in heaven is good. Whenever people sought to put him on a pedestal, he instead pointed beyond himself to the one he served, pointed to God. As elders-elect prepare for their service, somewhere along the way, they are so humbled that they are much less likely to say, "Look at me" and instead to say, "Look at God."

We return to the banks of the river Jordan, with John and Jesus. Let us wonder again, if we had been there on the day Jesus was baptized, if we would have heard God's voice. In Luke's version, the Father says to Jesus, "You are my son, the beloved." I like this way of telling the story. It reminds us that we all need God's affirmation. Without God's affirmation, we doubt that we can do what God calls us to do. Yes, I like Luke's version of the story.

In Matthew, the Father does not speak to Jesus. The father speaks to the crowd. "This is my son, the beloved." I like this way of telling the story. It reminds us that when God calls leaders, we need God's affirmation that they carry God's call. With God's affirmation, we are willing at least to give our leaders the benefit of the doubt. Yes, I like Matthew's way of telling the story.

Which do you like? Could both be true?

# Jesus in Whoville

## Luke 10.25-37

*This sermon was preached two days before Valentine's Day,
which happened also to be the congregation's annual Children's
Sabbath. It replicates the familiar rhythm and storyline of a Dr.
Seuss book to retell the Parable of the Good Samaritan.*

You have all heard of Whoville, where the Grinch you did meet,
and of green eggs and ham, which Sam would not eat,
and of Yertle the Turtle, and the Cat in the Hat,
you know all these stories, know all about that.

But I wonder,
  we wonder,
    you wonder, too,
      what might yet happen
        if Jesus met Seuss.

You know of the Lorax, you are aware of the sneetch,
but do you recall Jesus' story about thieves?

They crouched on the roadside, they hid behind walls,
they waited for travelers 'til the gray of nightfall
when they had leap to the open, attack from behind,
and they had pummel and trammel and be oh, so unkind.

Their victim was helpless, outnumbered, alone,
not many possessions, away from his home,
they had done their worst, they had stripped him clean,
the way that they left him is best called obscene.
Bloodied and battered, bruised and quite sore,
barely half conscious, very hard to ignore,
this wanderer languished, asleep in a ditch,
when a passerby noticed just a slight twitch.

"Thank God," that man thought, "to be seen by a pastor!
What could be better amidst such disaster,
than to be found by a man wearing a collar?"

He sat right up straight and started to holler.
But that person, that priest, that one they call Reverend,
he left our poor victim to an uncertain end.
Surprised and dejected, disappointed and sad,
our victim laid down again, hungry and mad.

More time went passing, an hour? Who knows?
Exhaustion was creeping from his head to his toes,
when far in the distance a new man came near,
a holy man, also, he had nothing to fear.
The Levite made eye contact, stared right at his pupil,
and still he walked on with barely a scruple.
The injuries worsened, his cuts, they burned,
while the likeliest helpers seemed quite unconcerned.

Now our story continues, but let us take a pause,
for Jesus told stories, but not without cause,
for he wanted his stories, wanted you and for me,
to enter his plotlines and in them to see,
ourselves, and others, the people we know,
and how we'd behave, how we might yet show,
what we believe, what we trust to be true,
if we'd been there that day – what would we do?

And do not get all uppity, self-righteous, or haughty,
for little has changed; we still can be naughty,
and yesterday's Levites and priests are still with us,
and still, right this moment, people fine and religious
keep finding a way, when seeing the needy,
to drive right on past, and I do mean quite speedy.
Levites and priests, they have a new name,
It is Baptist, and Catholic, and we are much the same.

So It is back to our story, the one told by Jesus
in order to claim us, to hold us, to seize us,
to capture our vision, our heart and our mind,
and inspire us to be Godlike: loving and kind.
So this lawyer coaxed Jesus, "What things must I do,
to earn righteousness, goodness, to be more like you?

I am sure it is hard work, requiring my labor,
but I am not very sure who you'd label my neighbor."

He is still where we left him, alone by the road,
when finally a passerby saw him and slowed,
and what's most surprising, unexpected, yet true,
is this helper's strange background, not at all much like you;
a foreigner, heretic, they called him Samaritan,
(now, finding a rhyme … I know: It is Claritin!)
Set silliness sailing, this story's quite serious,
our victim's new fortune left him delirious.

That stranger did hoist him upright top his horse,
and walked long beside him as a matter of course,
till they reached a quiet respite, where his care he did give,
anointing and wrapping and healing – he'd live!
He treated our victim with gentleness, care,
showed remarkable patience, and mercy, and shared.
The story, now finished, has answered the question,
the one that began it, which started our session,
when the lawyer asked Jesus, "Lord, what must I do,
to be gentle and righteous, to be something like you?"

We talk about love, we do it a lot,
especially at Valentines we say that love ought
to buy diamonds and rubies, chocolates and flowers,
when we say that love showers and showers and showers
its objects with objects, with testaments true,
which leaves me long wondering; precisely who's who?
Do givers and getters, the ones who exchange,
really get anything? Or do they arrange
what God has long given; It is wonderful, true,
to Valentines, Samaritans, wanderers, you!

If God meets us happily, wherever we go,
if God loves us wholly, from head down to toe,
if God weeps when we weep and God smiles when we smile,
then God too goes with us, mile to last mile.
And if God's greatest gift, at the top of the list,
is love's deepest expression, despite all the rifts

that exploit us, divide us, have long held us back,
then there is only one action that keep get us on track.

On this day made special especially for kids,
when teenagers, grade-schoolers, toddlers in bibs,
come worshiping, singing, wearing their finest,
standing before us despite all their shyness,
we are left wondering; what shall we say?
about blankets, and love, about God's unique way,
of loving us deeply, to show how It is true,
that following Jesus somehow changes you.

Remember Whoville, that mountainside village,
and that green Grinch, who tried to steal Christmas?
And do you remember, do you recall
that Grinch's problem? His heart was too small.
So children and grownups, sit straight and stand tall,
for Jesus comes calling, calling to all,
in Whoville and Fort Worth, in your heart and your home –
a neighbor's our neighbor wherever they roam –
'cross deserts or oceans or leaping tall walls.
Let our hearts keep on growing and never be small.

# Sin and Grace in Wonderland
## Luke 13:1-9

*I was taught to use personal illustrations in preaching with great caution, and that the best personal illustrations are those very commonly shared. I broke all the rules in this sermon, but somehow it seemed to work.*

Kids in my hometown, in the Texas Panhandle, take an eighth-grade trip. To the city. To Amarillo. At the end of each school year, we load ninety or one hundred excited teenagers into lumbering yellow school busses and head north for a day in Amarillo's Wonderland Park.

Now you must understand that Wonderland Park is not Disneyland. Far from it. There are no long lines or $5 drinks. Wonderland is more like one of those rickety carnivals that limp into your county fair, whose employees sport multiple tattoos and body piercings. Wonderland is like that, only the owners must have tired of traveling, so they put a fence around the place and hung a shingle and to kids who lived in my small hometown and who had never seen Disneyland anyway, Wonderland was, well, wonder land.

My cocky eighth grade class poured off those busses. We paraded through Wonderland's lighted arched gate, with its hundreds of light bulbs. Maybe a third were burned out or broken and I should have realized then that in Wonderland, the light shines a bit dimly in places. Still, nothing could have dimmed my day at that moment.

After all, we were grown now! My classmates and I would run around the park, without chaperones, for an entire afternoon. Completely alone. We were old enough to behave as adults, to be treated as adults. They could untie the knots, loose the binds, release their stranglehold, because we were trustworthy!

It was not yet noon when Keith Hunter[7] unzipped his backpack to show me that can of beer. I knew instantly that this single beer would spill disaster, and not just for those who drank it. This beer

---

[7] All names have been changed to protect the guilty.

would destroy those who merely saw it. Keith headed off, and like flies to watermelon a group formed behind him.

Now because my father is a Calvinist Presbyterian minister, I knew quite enough about fallen human nature to know exactly where they were going. They trailed off behind Keith Hunter toward a clump of trees behind a ride called *The Texas Twister.*

What those twelve boys expected to receive from their equal shares of a 12-ounce beer, I do not know. But word of their drunken escapade traveled like prairie fire and the truth escaped none of us. We were every one of us involved. If the principal, Mr. Wall, found out about that beer – and we knew he would – everyone who had merely heard about the beer but not come forward would be held as responsible as the unfortunate child who had popped the top.

I would like to tell you that I refused to drink that beer because of some grand moral conviction that underage minors should not. Or though less noble, I would even like to tell you that I did not drink that beer because I knew they were going to get caught. And that is true, too; I feared getting caught. But the honest reason I did not join my Budweiser buddies was that Marian Miller asked me to ride with her on *The Hammer.*

Now, there are dreams in life, and there are dreams. To be asked by Marian Miller to ride *The Hammer* was equivalent to being drafted by a professional football team, and I was not about to miss my place on the team.

There was only one problem; I was then going steady with Cindy Ray, a 7th grader. Many good things can be said about Cindy Ray. The most relevant to me at that moment was that she lived in an even smaller farming community than I did, and it is an easy 40-minute school bus ride from my hometown. I hoped that the distance would at least slow the news that I had ridden *The Hammer* with Marian Miller long enough for me to call Cindy and explain that the ride had meant nothing, though of course I hoped that it would.

I rode *The Hammer* with Marian Miller. Feeling guilty as I did, then, imagine my dilemma when next I was asked to ride *The Amazon* by none other than Martha, Marian's even more beautiful twin sister. Not only did I say yes; I bought Martha's ticket.

My adventure in Wonderland had to this point pushed me to the edge of the eighth grader's moral universe. The moral quandaries were stacking up: faithfulness, truth telling, the social contract. I had failed every test. What kind of person was I? I had been a good kid. How had I gone bad in two measly hours?

God knows us through and through, and if grace meets us anywhere, it meets us where we fail. I sat on a bench between the *Tunnel of Love* and the *House of Horrors* and contemplated what I had done. I tried to hide my terror from my friends, tried to act as if everything was normal and I was in control. But they were scared, too. After all, they knew about the beer. We were all in this together. Alison Johnson. Margaret Duke. Grant Lattimore. Bill Simpson.

It was then that we saw her, lurching toward us from the *Tunnel of Love*. Alone. It was Susan Johnson. Susan was by no means a popular girl. I am not sure which was more painfully obvious; that other kids did not much like Susan or that Susan did not much like herself. It hurt just to look at her. You could see in one glance a lifetime of neglect, a sordid tale of family dysfunction, a pitiful existence of poverty and abuse. In a small town, where you know everyone in your class from the first grade on, none of us had ever known how to react to Susan. So, we ignored her. Or we teased her, ostracized her. We eight years we had escorted Susan to her personal self-loathing.

Susan came closer.

She stopped at our bench.

We each looked down, or away, at the ground, at our feet, at anything to keep us from looking at Susan.

Susan spoke. "Will someone ride the roller coaster with me?"

I do not know what happened in that moment. Grace is like that. I know only that we rose to our feet and said that yes, we would ride the roller coaster with Susan Johnson. And we did. Each time the train stopped, we switched places so that all would have a chance to ride with Susan.

Other kids saw, too. At first, they pointed and laughed at us, and made fun of us for being with Susan, just as we had always done. But something happened to the naysayers, too, and they lined up as we left the roller coaster. They wanted to be a part of this grace. Ride to ride we went, all befriending Susan Johnson. It was as if the eighth-grade trip had become a corporate catharsis of repentance.

The bus horns signaled the end of our stay. We boarded and headed south, the class of '78.

Word of my betrayal reached Cindy before I did. She ended our burning love affair by admitting that her eye had been on Scott

Johnson all the while. Mr. Wall, the principal, called me to his office the following Monday. He knew about the beer. Why had not I turned the drunks in?

I did not know it then, as I sat in Mr. Wall's office, absorbing his words and lamenting Cindy's loss. I did not know it, but my eighth-grade class was a microcosm of human experience.

We were like some people who confronted Jesus one day. They reminded Jesus about some people Pilate had killed. They said those people got what was coming to them. More than that, they suggested that God allowed terrible things to happen to people to punish them. More even than that, these people implied that because bad things had not happened to them personally, they were better than people upon whom misfortune had fallen.

Which was how we had always thought about Susan Johnson. Susan was unattractive and unpleasant. Susan seemed not very intelligent. Susan wore old and ratty clothes and came to school unbathed and unkempt. We thought Susan had done something to deserve these things. And we thought we were better.

Jesus refused to let those people get away with that self-righteousness 2,000 years ago. He stood and faced them and told them that bad things happen to good people just as surely as good things happen to bad people. God does not say that faithful people won't have it tough. God promises instead that with God's help, we can be just tough enough to remain faithful despite it all.

And Jesus was not harsh, either. Jesus did not merely condemn their self-righteousness that day. Jesus gave them hope. He told them about a fig tree that was not bearing fruit. Still, the gardener refused to cut it down. He argued for one more year, a second chance, another shot. There is hope even for the self-righteous.

My trip to Wonderland had proven me a fruitless tree. Yet looking back, I cannot help but think that Susan Johnson provided one of my most memorable brushes with grace. My sense of failure, my betrayal of Cindy, my predicament over that can of beer, nothing kept God from loving me.

God loves us because love is who God is. It is what God does. God cannot help it. That is grace.

And grace begets grace. When Susan Johnson showed up to ride the roller coaster in Wonderland, the truest gift I could offer God was to respond with a mere fraction of the graciousness God had shown to me.

We may not grow the greatest figs. We may turn barren and ripe for the ax. Still, unbelievably, mysteriously, the master gardener offers us yet one more growing season, a second chance, another shot.

And that is just enough to keep us on the roller coaster in Wonderland.

# As God Prospers You: What God's Generosity Has to do with Yours

## Luke 15.11-32 and Genesis 9.1-3, 7-15a

*Stewardship is preaching's third rail, living as we do an age of skepticism of institutions. The stewardship preacher risks appearing as God's salesclerk. Yet, nowhere does the pulpit intersect more obviously with the day-to-day lives of American Christians than on the subject of being generous with God's provision.*

Stewardship season is upon us. What a misnomer. First, there is a better theological word than stewardship. More about that momentarily. Second, most congregations hardly spend a season discussing it. Most are content with a single Sunday, and a solitary Sunday sermon, as if the conversation is something akin to the dreaded annual flu shot.

Here is how I suspect most people view the conversation about sharing our money. A fine Presbyterian couple hold hands in first class on a flight to the Far East. Suddenly the Captain announces, "Ladies and Gentlemen, I have some very bad news. Our engines have ceased functioning. Our plane is going down. The good news is that I can see an island that should accommodate our landing. The bad news is that this island is uncharted. I cannot find it on our maps. The odds are good that we will never be rescued and will have to live on the island for the rest of our lives."

Mrs. Presbyterian turns to Mr. Presbyterians and asks, "Dear, did we turn off the oven?"

"Of course," he replies.

He asks her, "Are our life insurance policies paid up?"

"Yes, of course," she responds.

"Darling, did you get the pledge card to the church?"

"Oh no," she replies, "I forgot!"

Mr. Presbyterian replies, "Thank God. They will find us for sure."

To many, the church's stewardship teaching sounds merely like an appeal to meet the church's budget. We talk about staff costs and utilities, about mission commitments and building needs. We talk about the church's need to receive and rarely do we mention the individual's need to give. And only rarely do we talk about God.

I want to talk about God. I have chosen two passages about God. One of them you might expect. The other, maybe not. Both remind us that God is generous.

So come back with me to the story of Noah and his family. They build the ark. They gather the animals. They drift for days, for weeks. Finally, the waters recede and they are on dry ground.

If the flood story is a divine/human breakup, the encounter we read today is the makeup scene. It is the reconciliation. God is changed. God is different. God promises, never again. "Never again shall there be a flood to destroy the earth."

Here is the kicker. Earlier in the Biblical story, back, way back, at the creation, God gives Adam and Eve all green things to eat. God gives human beings, God's image-bearers upon the earth, all plants to be eaten for food (Genesis 1.29).

Now, at the conclusion of the Noah story, God says something different, gives something more. Now, God says to Noah and his family, "Be fruitful and multiply, and fill the earth. Every moving thing that lives shall be food for you; and just as I gave you the green plants, *I give you everything.*"

Did you hear it? God's provision has expanded. God gives Adam and Eve all green things. God gives Noah's family plants and animals. Everything. God gives everything!

Then God promises that never again shall a flood wash away life on earth. God makes a covenant. The sign of that covenant is the rainbow. We teach church school children that a rainbow in the sky is a visual reminder of God's love. The text has it that rainbows prohibit another worldwide flood. But there is more. Rainbows actually promise God's universal provision.

God gives everything. God holds nothing back. That is who God is, what God does. God is generous.

This is what we are thinking about this morning, about God's generosity. So, in addition to God's generosity in the Noah story we are also remembering the Parable of the Prodigal Son. It is probably the best remembered of Jesus's parables. You know it by heart.

A younger son demands the early division of the family estate. He leaves with his inheritance and quickly blows it on wine, women, and song. Updated, that is sex, drugs, and rock and roll. Now, he has the audacity to come home.

The father sees him from afar. Overjoyed that his son has come home, he pulls up his robe – a scandalous act for a Jewish patriarch – and runs to meet his wayward son at the property's edge. All is forgiven. Grace overwhelms forgiveness. "Get my boy a new robe. Put a ring on his finger. Kill the fatted calf. Invite the neighbors."

The parable might be misnamed. We call it the Parable of the Prodigal Son, but it is not really about the younger son. The word prodigal means wasteful, reckless, extravagant, uncontrolled. The son is not ultimately the prodigal character in the story. The father is. Against all reason, his generosity is positively reckless, wholly extravagant, completely uncontrolled. The story is about the father's generosity.

Not everyone likes such wasteful generosity. The older son certainly does not. He has never left the farm. He has served faithfully without question or complaint. He is in the fields when the scallywag skulks in and he must hear from a servant about the banquet goings on. And he is furious. He will not join the party.

If we remember the makeup scene in the Noah story, we might call the final scene in the Parable of the Prodigal Son the decision scene. The older brother has a decision to make. The father and the older son meet at the party's entrance. The older son complains that never before has the father been so generous with him.

The father's response says it all. The father's response hits hard, speaks loudly, shouts, actually, because if you are like me, of all the characters in the story, you are most like the older brother. The father looks to the older brother and says, "Son, you are always with me. All that is mine is yours."

All that is mine is yours. This parable is paradigmatic to the entire Gospel of Christ. It is emblazoned with Jesus' central and most important message.

Yes, God welcomes even the sinner home. And even more basically, God is generous. God gives everything. God holds nothing back. "All that is mine is yours."

Generosity is God's foundational characteristic. No one worships a stingy God. If "God loves a cheerful giver," humanity loves a generous God. However else our perceptions of the divine differ, generosity is God's universally appreciated attribute. People are drawn to God for dramatically different reasons. For some, God is first loving. For others, God is most importantly forgiving. Some prefer a God who is just, or merciful, or gracious, or kind, or creative.

What's your favorite divine characteristic? No matter your preferred divine attribute, what finally evokes your passion is God's reckless and extravagant generosity in sharing it.

I bet you have seen that old Children's Moment about stewardship. I am a bit embarrassed to admit it, but I have used it. It is the one where we call the kids up then pull ten apples from a grocery sack. We count the apples. We explain that one apple goes back to the church and we get to keep the other nine. "What a generous God," we declare. "God lets us keep nine apples."

Here is the problem with that Children's Moment. The truth is much better than that. God lets us keep all ten apples. "I give you everything," God echoes from Noah. God promises all of us older brothers and older sisters, "All that is mine is yours."

God is that generous.

What is more, the entire Biblical narrative is the sacred saga of God's sequential generosities. As God's provision multiplies from Eden to Noah, God will give yet more. The Bible story is a dynamic, successive adding on of God's good gifts, one atop the other. It is a tale of relentless, dynamic generosity. If one gift does not do, God will give another. Then another. God gives the creation, and the covenant, and then prophets to remind and inspire. God gives the law and the land. The Jewish story, and then the Christian story, is the saga of a parent so compelled by love, so possessed of grace, so hungry for relationship that there seems no end to the parent's willingness to give.

And, there is no limit to the parent's capacity to give. Until, that is, the parent gives all that he has.

We have arrived at the essence of the Christian faith. In the center of time, at the turning point for all meaning, God gives yet again. This time, God's generosity knows no constraint. It is limitless and expansive, extravagant and reckless. God gives God's very self. God is completely, wholly, irreversibly, undeniably, irretrievably, inevitably, unexpectedly, oh-so-graciously and eternally – generous. It is what God does. It is who God is.

I have called this sermon "As God Prospers You: What God's Generosity Has to do with Yours." Do not worry! I am not a prosperity preacher. You will never guess from where I stole that word, *prospers*? It comes from the 1946 edition of *The Book of Common Worship* of the old Presbyterian Church in the United States of America. It appears in one of the questions asked of kids when they confirm. Here is the entire question:

> *Do you promise to make diligent use of the means of grace, to share faithfully in the worship and service of the Church, to give of your substances as the Lord may prosper you, and to give your whole heart in the service of Christ and His kingdom throughout the world?"*

Imagine, the audacity to ask fourteen-year-olds to give of their substance as the Lord may prosper them. "As God Prospers You: What God's Generosity Has to do with Yours."

We are so very tempted to think of our stewardship efforts as mere fundraising. We assume that the entire affair has first to do with meeting the church's budget. We suspect that it is about salaries and insurance and light bills and throw in a few mission projects to be safe.

This conversation includes these things. That is true.

But it is about more, a great deal more. It is about something much more basic and more holy and more deeply, beautifully, authentically more. In its holiest sense – that is to say in its most practical sense – our stewardship efforts are nothing less than the organized summons to participate in the very generosity of God. Every letter you receive in this season, filling in your family's pledge card, every worship testimonial you hear, has to do with our congregation's shared effort to inspire one another towards greater trust in God's provision and then, then, then to funnel that generosity into the world.

This fall, in our stewardship campaign, may you fall into God's generous arms and find there such provision and grace that you are compelled to pour open your heart and your substance. We will get to the church's budget and mission soon enough. First, what do you need to give in order to express your spiritual convictions?

# Dances with Wolves

## Luke 16:1-13

*I spend more time on basic exegesis in this sermon than I normally do, but wrestling with the complexities of the texts bears great fruit.*

This a difficult parable, a perplexing parable. Jesus tells it to his disciples. That is worth noting because mostly in Luke, Jesus offers parables to his opponents. They always at him, harrumphing because Jesus spends time with sinners and no-accounts of various kinds.

In Luke's previous chapter Jesus has plopped at his opponents' feet three of our favorite parables. In one, the shepherd risks everything to retrieve one lost sheep. In the next parable, the angels rejoice when a woman finds a single lost coin. Finally, the prodigal son returns to a welcome party and the father's outrageous love.

We love these parables. God's love is for everyone, even the unexpected people, even those we would not think deserve God's love. These are reassuring parables, comforting parables, grace-ful parables.

So unexpectedly Luke kicks off his 16th chapter with a parable for loyalists, for Jesus' disciples. A rich man is being swindled. An audit has caught his employee red handed. He has cooked the books. The rich man does what any sensible business person would do. He fires his crooked manager.

The story is not over, though. The employee is too weak for manual labor and too proud to beg, so he goes to Plan D. Behind his boss's back – yet again! – he visits his boss's clients. He slashes their debts. He makes back room deals. He scratches their backs so that, when the time comes, they will scratch his.

His behavior is strategic. It is cynical. Self-serving. Machiavellian.

And what does the rich man do when he hears about it? He commends his manager! He congratulates him! Can you even believe it?

What, exactly, are we to learn from *that*?

Truth is, scholars have as many opinions about the meaning of this parable as politicians have opinions about the economy. That should come as no surprise, of course. This parable was so perplexing from the beginning that even the gospel writer seems uncertain what to make of it. That is why we get three "so what" statements at the end of the parable. Biblical parables often work that way. Jesus tells the parable. That is the *what*. Then the Bible gives us the *so what*, a brief summary or explanation.

This parable has three *so whats*.

"Whoever is faithful in a very little is faithful also in much."

"If you have not been faithful with dishonest wealthy, who will entrust you the true riches?"

"You cannot serve God and wealth."

There are at least three sermons here. And not one of them seems clearly connected to the idea that Jesus seems to praise the behavior of a greedy and crooked underling. "Make friends for yourselves," Jesus commands, "by means of dishonest wealth so that when it is gone, they may welcome you into the eternal homes."

It makes no sense, until, we get at the original language, the Greek, and we learn that "dishonest wealth" is not the only translation. It is not even the best translation. "Dishonest wealth" is better translated "the wealth of this age," or better yet, "the money of this unrighteous age."

"Make friends for yourselves by means of the money of this unrighteous age."

It is not the money that is dishonest. It is the age. The time. The context. The culture! It is the culture which is unrighteous and devastating.

And this we understand. Who in this sanctuary does not feel the inner conflict between discipleship and citizenship in this changing culture?

The sermon title is a play on an old movie title, *Dances with Wolves*. The movie is about a nineteenth century cavalry officer who becomes friendly with a tribe of Lakota Sioux. More than friendly, in the end, actually. He becomes one of them. He joins the tribe. He leaves behind his Anglo ways and becomes a Great Plains Indian.

His new family names him Dances with Wolves because he did. Through patience and humility this man worked his way into a pack of wolves. Animals notoriously closed and careful, aggressive and violent, welcome a strange and different creature into their pack. He danced with wolves.

Earlier in Luke, Jesus says this to his disciples. "Go on your way. See, I am sending you out like lambs into the midst of wolves."

43

So this is what is going on in this awkward parable of the shrewd manager, the parable of the unjust steward. Jesus is sending his disciples into the midst of wolves.

These questions must be answered. How will disciples survive the encounter? How do we live Gospel values in a culture in some ways hostile to us? How do we dance with wolves and not be eaten by them, or even worse, join the pack?

Jesus is not praising dishonest managers. Jesus is not lifting shrewd and crooked people as examples of godly behavior. We are not about to burst out of this sanctuary and study up on Michael Milken and Ken Lay to get where God wants us going.

Jesus is suggesting something altogether different. Learn *from* them, Jesus says. Do not *become* them.

Think about people who deal shrewdly in the world. You know the sort. They wake up every morning ready to close the deal, to chase the buck. They plot, and they prepare. They check the market and they cut the corners and they drool over the next deal. They work the angles. They cut the corners. They glad-hand and they back-scratch. They look out for number one. They cheat their mothers if there is a buck in it.

Remember *Cheers*, the old television show? Remember Norm, the affable stool sitter? Norm knew about wolves. They asked Norm how he was doing one day, and this is what he said. "It is a dog-eat-dog world out there and I am wearing milk bone underwear."

Wolves. Pack animals. All for one and one for all, until one can gain the edge.

Jesus is saying, Look at them. Learn from them!

Why, if you put some small portion of that strategic passion in service not to greed, but in service to the Gospel, imagine the difference you will make in the world. Look at those go-getters, those movers-and-shakers, those wheeler-dealers. Look at their passion. Imagine that passion in service to something noble, something pure, something divine.

That is what Jesus is saying. Dance with wolves. Learn from them, but do not become like them. Watch them, but do not be changed into them. Be shrewd for the gospel; wily, energetic, passionate. But do not be changed.

Dance with wolves, but do not let them name the tune.

That has always been the church's greatest challenge, you know. How do we minister to a culture without becoming just like the culture? Paul commanded us not to "be conformed to this world," but "to be transformed by the renewing of [our] minds, so that [we] may discern what is the will of God — what is good and acceptable and perfect" (Romans 12.2). Sometimes we get it right. Sometimes, we blow it.

We come to think that big is necessarily better, and that popularity equals righteousness. That is one of the basic instincts behind the mega church movement. Critical mass, they call it. Full auditoriums. Fender benders in the packed parking lot. Faithfulness is measured in attractiveness.

That is a cultural value, not necessarily a Gospel value.

Years ago, one of my church members told me that she and her husband had left their country club. Oh, they had the money. She simply became embarrassed that they spent more at the country club than they contributed to the ministries of her church. She applied a Gospel value over a cultural value.

Dance with wolves, but you name the tune.

Would not you say that a congregation's faithfulness to God is measured by its passionate witness to God's ongoing presence in the world, to God's bringing dignity to people who have none, to God's gathering people who otherwise would not be caught dead together, to God's healing people of hurts they thought beyond cure?

That is what Jesus says, in Luke. He eats with sinners and cures people and feeds people. That is why his opponents are always after him. They are appalled. Jesus rewards sinners and outcasts with life's most valuable gifts. Nurture. Grace. Belonging. Dignity. Love. Forgiveness. And of these priceless gifts, not one of them can be bought. They cannot be sold or bartered or stolen or swindled. These gifts are intangible.

So "make friends for yourselves by means of the money of this unrighteous age so that when it is gone, they may welcome you into the eternal homes."

"So that when it is gone."

That shrewd manager, that wheeler-dealer, that backscratching glad hander always primed with a quid pro quo – all that energy, all that intellect, all that passion devoted to schemes about stuff that does not last. "So that when it is gone."

Learn from him, Jesus says, but do not become like him, because you are playing for the long run. This world, it is passing away. God's kingdom is coming forever.

# Stuff Happens

## Acts 1:15-17, 21-26

*If I could erase misleading religious aphorisms from the cultural vocabulary, I would remove this one first; "everything happens for a reason." Here's why.*

Years ago, a friend and church member cut a very interesting deal with God. Our congregation was raising pledges to expand its building. My friend hatched an idea. Each week he bought a lottery ticket with the same numbers, derived from his family's birthdays. Bob was convinced that if he promised half the jackpot to the church's building fund, God would award him a winning ticket. He imagined his hero status when making this someday gift, and his only request of the church would be a stone plaque above the Fellowship Hall door bearing the winning numbers. Bob was teasing, of course.

I think.

If he was serious, he would hardly have stood alone. We do it often, do we not? I do not mean trying to cut quid-pro-quo deals with God, though that is common enough. I mean that we look for God's will in the strangest places.

Some look to events, believing that God "has a plan" and that "everything happens for a reason." Some look to the stars, convinced that astrological positions will guide their lives and choices. Some look to other individuals, and they glom onto people whose confidence clears the clouds of their own befuddlement. And some play the lottery. Or they roll the dice. Or they cast lots.

Picture this imaginary meeting of a congregational Nominating Committee. It gathers behind closed doors on a weekday morning. The coffee is poured. The committee members pray, asking God's will and wisdom. Committee members are searching for an elder to complete an unexpired term on the Session. They have narrowed the field to two, both fine people, people who worship regularly and pray obviously, people who volunteer at Habitat for Humanity, who sit on committees. These two have seen and done it all. Then, the committee chair reaches into her purse and pulls out two dice, looted from *Monopoly* at home. "We will throw the dice," she says. "If the number is 6 or under, candidate A gets the nod. If the dice give us 7 or more, we will go with candidate B."

What would you think if your Nominating Committee chose our leaders like that? They would not have to use the dice, of course. They could draw the short straw. Or pick the high card from a deck of Bicycle playing cards. Maybe chant eeny meeny miny mo.

Seems a bit random, eh? Have you seen that, people so hungry for God's will that no matter what happens, they attribute an outcome to God?

I love *The Simpsons*, television's longest running situation comedy. Sometimes *The Simpsons* is surprisingly theological. Listen to one of Homer Simpson's prayers:

> *"Dear Lord: For the first time in my life, everything is absolutely perfect just the way it is.*
>
> *So here is the deal: You freeze everything the way it is, and I won't ask for anything more.*
>
> *If that is OK, please give me absolutely no sign. OK, deal. In gratitude, I present you this offering of cookies and milk.*
>
> *If you want me to eat them for you, give me no sign.*
>
> *Thy will be done."*

It is hilarious when Homer does it. He makes comically apparent what we see in the real world. It is honorable and beautiful to seek God's will when making decisions. It is Christlike to say, "not my will but yours be done" (Luke 22.42). And seeking God's will, well, it is an interesting task. Do we see God's providence, or do we scour our lives for circumstantial coincidence?

What is coincidence, and what is providence, and how can we tell the difference? I ask the question because the disciples asked it, the original disciples, all of them. By the time we reach the first chapter of Acts, the disciples are down to eleven. You remember who is missing. Judas betrayed Jesus. Then, he died a horrible death, or took his own life, depending on which gospel you read. Either way, Judas is gone.

The remaining band of brothers ache over Judas. How could one of their own betray Jesus? Never mind, of course, that they had all betrayed Jesus, denying him, abandoning him. In a way, the perplexity of Judas is the complexity of complicity, the reality that each disciple has betrayed Jesus if only to a lesser degree. Why did Judas do it? Was it coincidence, or providence?

Coincidence describes events which are statistically unlikely. Providence is the idea that God is directing events as they unfold.

Coincidence is "A sequence of events that although accidental seems to have been planned or arranged." [8] Providence is the idea that God did the arranging and the planning.

Which was Judas? Peter thinks he knows. Judas was providence. "The scripture had to be fulfilled," he says. And with this mystery explained, the apostles must face their problem. They are one short. Twelve is a Biblical number, mirroring the tribes of Israel. They must fill the unexpired term.

So the apostles rack their brains for others who have known Jesus from the start of his ministry. Notice that even though they cast lots to make their final choice, they also have minimum requirements. The winning candidate will have been with them since Jesus' baptism, and he must become a willing witness to the resurrection. The apostles sort the field to two candidates. Then, in one of the weirdest moments in the New Testament, they cast lots. Maybe the writing team at *The Simpsons* had this passage in mind when Homer presented his cookies to God. The apostles cast lots. Matthias is chosen. Chosen by God? Chosen by chance? Providence? Coincidence?

We risk, I suspect, we risk assuming that because scripture records a practice, it recommends the practice. Approves it. Advises it. Sometimes, however, stories are recorded in scripture without prejudice. They are told without comment, reported like a neutral reporter would tell them, "just the facts, ma'am." The Bible includes exhortations – "here, do this." The Bible includes prohibitions – "here, do not do this."

This story is neither. This story is, well, a story. That the disciples cast lots for Matthias does not mean that our Nominating Committee should begin throwing dice. Our committee meets weekly, you know, in deep prayer and reflection. And research. They bring to the nominating table all the facts that their eyes can see, and their minds recall, and our church's database has recorded.

---

[8] *The American Heritage® Dictionary of the English Language*, Fourth Edition copyright ©2000 by Houghton Mifflin Company. Updated in 2009. Published by Houghton Mifflin Company.

The question faced by that Nominating Committee is the same question faced by those apostles back then, which is the same question we face now, day in and week out. Coincidence, or providence? How can we know the will of God?

Are you ready for the answer? Wait for it, wait for it ... here it is. Sometimes we cannot. We do not. Try as we might, the mystery of God is not always altogether obvious in the events unfolding around us.

This answer – that we are not always able to discern the distinction between random chance and divine movement – that answer will never satisfy those who seek absolute certitude in their religion. This is a hard word for those who want the world, and God, on clear and certain terms. For those seeking to expel doubt from their faith, this is a difficult answer. But you know about the opposite of doubt. The opposite of doubt is not faith. The opposite of doubt is certainty. If everything is certain, faith is not necessary. The Matthias story reminds us that faith requires trust.

Faith is the trust that God is active in the world, and though we do not always see it, our life is about looking.

Was Matthias the right choice? We do not know. Matthias is never mentioned again. Not once. Maybe he lapsed into obscurity because he did nothing important, and maybe he did nothing important because he was a bad selection. Maybe Matthias is never mentioned against because of the shadow into which he stepped. I cannot name Benedict Arnold's successor, either.

Perhaps the Mathias story is not about Mathias at all, but about the apostles, about the apostles' bold and illogical conviction that God is vibrantly active in the world working God's purposes out. The Matthias story stands as bold testament to the unexpected Christian conviction that God is alive and active in our lives, beneath and within and winsomely present, somehow completing the restoration of the world. Convinced of this, the Christian task is seeking and following God's movement in the world.

This does not mean that everything which happens, God has willed to happen. Sometimes, stuff happens. And this is true not only in Nominating Committee meetings. Sometimes, cancer happens. Sometimes, cars crash. Hurricanes howl. Bullets obliterate. Bullies bully. Stuff happens.

And graciously God is more steadfastly reliable than tossing dice or casting lots. God's will, though mysterious, is available. God's presence, too. Through prayer. With others who pray. In community. We have just named the recipe for seeking the will of God, the mind of Christ: prayer, partners, and church.

In the end, the apostles' example serves us well. God still speaks, and we are wise to gather with others who are listening. Our lives are piloted by the conviction that God's will is worth seeking, even if sometimes we are uncertain that we know it.

# Spirit Happens

## Romans 8.22-27 and Acts 2.1-21

*This sermon, preached on Pentecost 2018, followed news stories of Ebola's return, yet another school shooting, and the start of yet another historically hot spring.*

Now this is Pentecost Sunday. Today the Spirit descends as divided tongues of fire. The Spirit drops on the Apostles and everyone gathered, and no matter their homeland, regardless their native language, everyone understands the message about Jesus.

Today, around the world, Pentecostals are waving their arms. They are dancing in the aisles and shouting alleluias. They are ecstatic. They are euphoric. They are breaking out in glossolalia, the speaking in tongues.

But we, we are Presbyterians. We are a cerebral people, a dignified people. Our worship is regal and orderly. You know you are a Presbyterian if the Holy Spirit comes upon you with power, and you scratch your chin, turn to your neighbor, and quietly whisper, "Hmmm. I have never thought about it that way."

If we took a survey on our favorite person of the Trinity, my guess is that the Father would garner 50% of the vote. Jesus would place second at 40%. Finally, the Holy Spirit might draw 10% of the Presbyterian ballot. (Followers of Jesus have a natural way of sorting themselves out. Spirit people do not tend to settle in Presbyterian churches. That said, you Spirit people are more than welcome here. God knows we need you.)

All of this means that Pentecost is a tad awkward for Presbyterians. God's winsome and uncontrollable spirit enlivening a Presbyterian worship service is about as likely as an African American preaching at a Prince Harry and Meghan Markle's royal wedding.

Oh. Wait. God works in mischievous ways. It could happen.

I suppose our Pentecost reluctance has to do with more than our sense of decorum. Oh, we hear the Pentecost story about tongues of fire, about people dreaming dreams and having visions. And then, the story rushes to our brains, and the questions fly. We have no problem believing that God still speaks to people, though we prefer it when God's voice is corroborated. We need multiple witnesses. That is why we believe in group decision making. We take a lot of votes.

We have no problem with the idea that God still speaks to people, and we trust that the Holy Spirit is the messenger. That is what Pentecost is all about. God speaks. God gives us a message, the good news, and the world needs to hear some good news.

So God's Holy Spirit is both messenger and inspiration. People get fired up. Excited. Exuberant. They spread out and fan the flames and tell the story and the Spirit just keeps on coaxing, keeps on inspiring, and the captives are liberated and the downtrodden are lifted up. Yes indeed, that Holy Spirit is how God speaks to us and leads us on.

But there is more, and it is worth thinking about. If the book of Acts has the Spirit descending and inspiring, the book of Romans has the Spirit ascending and listening hard. Listening for our prayers. Taking our prayers to God. In Acts, the Spirit brings God's message to us, and through us, to the world. In Romans, the Spirit takes our message to God.

Imagine that. God speaks. But God listens, too.

Do you doubt that sometimes? Do you wonder if God is really listening?

Ebola is back, in the Congo. Three confirmed cases in a city of over a million. Imagine what happens if that virus gets loose in an urban setting. God, are you listening?

94 degrees on May 19. The whole earth is warming. Your creatures are making it worse. God, are you listening?

23 shooting victims in Santa Fe, Texas. 10 dead. Yet another school shooting. God, are you listening?

Do you wonder sometimes? Come, Holy Spirit, come. Come not only with God's message of good news. Come also and take our prayers with you, back into the heart of God.

Sometimes, I am so overwhelmed by the news that I am not sure what to pray. Does that happen to you?

When I visit people in the hospital, I ask the patient for what to pray. We can never presume to know what another wants prayed. We must ask. Sometimes, the patient looks up from her bed and knows immediately exactly what her prayer should be.

But other times, there is silence. Sometimes the patient is silent. It is not an awkward silence. It is an honest silence. Sometimes we do not know for what to pray.

I relish those moments. There is a decency in silence that sometimes trumps the confidence of words. I have many times sat bedside, holding a hand, in complete quiet, because neither I nor the patient knew what to say to God.

"Likewise," the Apostle Paul says, "the Spirit helps us in our weakness; for we do not know how to pray as we ought."

Have you been there? Have you been tongue-tied before God?

"But that very Spirit," Paul continues, "that very Spirit intercedes with sighs too deep for words."

The Spirit meets us in silence. The Spirit intercedes. The Spirit sighs.

The virus is spreading, and among the least fortune. Sigh.

The Earth is warming, and we are contributing to it. Sigh.

Our kids are scared in their schools. Sigh.

> *"We know that the whole creation has been groaning in labor pains until now; and not only the creation, but we ourselves, who have the first fruits of the Spirit, [we] groan inwardly while we wait for adoption, the redemption of our bodies."*

That is how Paul puts it. The Spirit sighs and the people groan. We know that things are not the way they should be, not yet. We are in the delivery room, waiting for the birth. In the 19th verse, just before the bit we read today, Paul says that the entire creation waits in "eager expectation." But the Greek there, it loses something in translation. What is translated "eager expectation" means literally to "crane one's neck." Picture a kid peeking around the corner.

"Hmmm. I have never thought of it like that before."

Craning one's neck. Peeking around the corner. We cannot wait for what is next. Because it is going to be good. God promises.

"On earth as it is in heaven." That is our regular prayer. And we, we are an in-between people. We stand firmly and consciously amidst things as they actually are. No Pollyannas needed. No delusions. No denials. No false optimism. We see things as they are. The Spirit sighs and the people groan because we know that we are live in the in-between.

Martin Luther King said famously that "the arc of the moral universe is long, but it bends towards justice." Paul says that "we wait for adoption. For in hope we were saved."

In hope we were saved. Saved. In hope.

When the news leaves us in stunned silence,
when the doctor drops on us the feared diagnosis,
when our supervisor hands us the dreaded pink slip,
we cling to God's omnipotent hope.

When the highway patrol calls at midnight,
when our kids make choices from which we cannot protect
    them,
when love evades us,
we cling to God's omnipotent hope.

We are the in-between people.

We live and witness on the way to something better, something perfect, something holy. We can see the city on the hill, there, just there, off in the distance, and in that city, viruses are no more. There, the creation rejoices in its restoration and health. There, kids do not even think about taking guns to school. For in hope we were saved.

Pentecost is not only about receiving a message to be shared. It is also about receiving a message to be prayed.

*Sigh.*

Come, Holy Spirit.
Come upon us with tongues of fire.
And also, meet us in the silence. Teach us to pray.

Hold us in hope, that the world will see in us the fiery confidence that by your grace, we are all of us headed to a better day.

In Jesus we ask it, O Holy Spirit. Come to us and pray through us. Amen.

# Who's Your Genius?

## Acts 2:1-21

*Another Pentecost sermon, this sermon was intended to relocate the gifts of the Holy Spirit from the personal and private to the shared and universal.*

You know by now the meaning of Pentecost. *Pente* – as in Pentagon, pentagram. Pente means five. Pentecost is fifty days past Easter. That is where Pentecost gets its name.

Pentecost is one of the few Sundays when Presbyterians allow themselves to display our most brightly colored paraments and stoles; you know, the *red* ones. Red is vibrant. Red is passionate. Red is provocative. Think about it. "The Lady in Red." Some cities have "red light districts." Several years ago, religious women everywhere read that bestseller, *The Red Tent*.

If people turn green with envy, people get passionate over red. When people go out for a wild night, they "paint the town red." So let us admit it from the get-go; as Presbyterians, Pentecost is frightening stuff.

Maybe you heard the song by that Texas songwriter Robert Earle Keene:

> *Still, I get restless and drive into town*
> *I cruise once down Main Street and turn back around*
> *It's crazy but God knows I do not act my age*
> *Like an old desperado who paints the town beige.* [9]

Paint the town beige. That is us! Presbyterian faith is not Fire Engine Red. It's beige.

That first Pentecost was Fire Engine Red. Jesus is resurrected from the dead. Christ is ascended into heaven. Now, the disciples wait.

That is when it happens. Everyone is there. Parthians. Medes. Elamites. Everybody. Remember the Old Testament story about the Tower of Babel? God's people wanted to elevate themselves to God,

---

[9] Robert Earle Keene, *Paint the Town Beige* (Nashville: Sugar Hill Records, 1993), www.azlyrics.com.

to become like God, so they built a tower to span the distance. But we are not God, so in that story God divides people into linguistic families, splits us up, spreads us out, and we are unable to understand one another, unable to work together. We remember that story every time we say that someone is speaking babble. Babble is synonymous with *indecipherable, impenetrable, meaningless.*

They are all there – Parthians, Medes, Elamites, everybody! – when it happens. The wind crashes and bangs. The house where the disciples are sitting is filled. Then "divided tongues, as of fire" appear out of nowhere. Upon each of the disciples – snack, crack, pop – a tongue settles. Onlookers assume they are drunk. But on this they agree, at this they are all amazed; residents of Mesopotamia, Judea and Cappadocia understand what the disciples say. What God had done at Babel, God reverses at Jerusalem. The chaos of Babel is set in order in Christ. And that is why we get out the red stoles at Pentecost, and that is why we call this in some way the birthday of the Church.

If Jesus is the "what," if the resurrection is the "so what," Pentecost is the "now what." "Now," God says, "go and live in Christ. And invite all peoples to do the same." The message is true and understandable in every language. In Christ there is no East or West. Jesus is for everyone.

The Church is still interpreting and living into this story, of course. Some Christians believe that the disciples became unexplainably multi-lingual that day. They assume that the disciples began speaking different languages, literally.

Others see in the story a different message. It was not so much that the disciples suddenly spoke in different tongues. What was new was in the *hearing*; suddenly, God's Spirit enabled people to understand this new message – that Jesus was for everyone.

And that question – is the meaning in the speaking or in the hearing, is the message in the tongue or in the ear, is the point of Pentecost the disciples' newfound talent or is the point of Pentecost found outside of us – that problem is worth pondering.

I am a fan of TED Talks. TED stands for technology, education, and design. For over twenty years now, TED talks have invited the most creative, influential, and intelligent thinkers in the world to present their ideas in a single speech. There is only one rule, apparently. The speeches cannot last longer than eighteen minutes.

Not long-ago Elizabeth Gilbert delivered a TED Talk. [10] Gilbert wrote that runaway bestseller *Eat, Pray, Love*. For her TED Talk Gilbert chose to describe the creative process. She began, imagine this, in ancient Greece and Rome. She reminded her audience that the ancients did not believe that human beings are innately creative, that great ideas emerge from within us. Instead, the Greeks believed that the creative spirit came to human beings from outside of us. *Daemons*, they called them. Some *daemons* were benevolent, were good. Some were malevolent, bad. You will recognize that word as resembling "demon," which is the Biblical word describing a malevolent spirit.

The Romans absorbed and changed the concept, calling these attendant spirits not *daemons* but rather *geniuses*. Geniuses were flitting forces which arrived unexpectedly to inform and inspire. Geniuses were external, outside of us, uncontrollable entities which could not be conjured, but who arrived without warning to gift recipients with information and wisdom that otherwise, they could never have created on their own. People were the beneficiaries of these geniuses – unseen, mysterious, and winsome.

This idea weathered the centuries, until the Renaissance. The Renaissance put the human being in the center of the universe. Mystery was out; knowledge was in. Mysticism was replaced by logic and reason. Rational humanism leaves little space for winsome spirits. Then, Gilbert argues, for the first time people began saying not that they "have" a genius but rather that they "are" a genius.

That shift is a big deal. It is momentous. It is a crucial swing in thinking because it moves the focus away from a wisdom external to self and places it within oneself.

Which is why Pentecost matters so deeply, maybe even more now than it did then. Only by remembering that the greatest wisdom comes from outside of us are we able to understand the idea that only God can release the greatest wisdom already residing deep within us.

Let me repeat that. Only by remembering that the greatest wisdom comes from outside of us are we able to understand the idea that only God can release the greatest wisdom already residing deep within us.

---

[10] Broadcast February 2009,
https://www.ted.com/talks/elizabeth_gilbert_on_genius.

Remember, in Luke, when Jesus says, that "the kingdom of God is within you?" Some have taken that to mean that human beings are in ourselves sufficient. Some have taken it to mean that the surest path to meaning and purpose is to explore ourselves, to know ourselves most deeply. Some have taken it to mean that by use of our God-given curiosity and intellect, we may rely solely upon our knowledge and tools of reason and wind our way to satisfaction and wholeness. Some have understood this to mean that all meaning and purpose is to be found within us. Some believe that life's ultimate significance can only be found by going deep and posing only to oneself all questions about who we are and what we are for and where we are going.

What deceptive and dead-end explanations of humanity. What pressure! What arrogance! Because these ideas are only half the truth.

We discover the greatest purpose and meaning in life when what is most deeply within us meets what is most authentically God, and that requires waiting upon God. Over and over. What happens at Pentecost is a vibrant assertion of two things. First, the seeds of our purpose do lie within us. And two, they await release.

What is more, it turns out that my meaning, my purpose, and my direction are incredibly personal, but they are not private, because they are interwoven with yours. Turns out, the Spirit descends not simply to individuals, but to individuals gathered, gathered together, gathered for a shared meaning, gathered for a corporate cause. We are together the body of Christ and individually we are members of him.

Pentecost is the heavenly and mysterious declaration that our reason for being is discovered when we wait upon the divine and offer ourselves willingly in obedience to it. Together.

That this truth is so readily displayed at the Spirit's winsome presence at Pentecost reminds us of another great truth, that to be most wholly ourselves we need not only one another; we need one another in the Church. The Church. The body of Christ. The Spirit calls us into the Church. The Spirit gives us identity within the Church. The Spirit uses us together in the Church that we might together be a witness of God's ongoing reconciliation in the world.

Oh, that Holy Spirit. She is our genius. She arrives without warning. We cannot control her. We can never conjure her. She is sovereign, with a divine mind of her own. Without her, we are left to wander for anything for matters, and with her, we discover everything that matters.

We *are* not geniuses. We *have* a genius. We share her, a common genius, a divine, mysterious, winsome Spirit of God. In the Spirit of God, we discover our truest selves, our deepest purpose, who we are and what we are for.

She calls us, together.

She calls us together.

And now, she sends us forth with the clarifying, unifying, world changing message of Jesus Christ.

# What's the Good Word?

## John 1.1-5, 14 and Colossians 1.11-20

*This sermon — an unusual sermon for a second Sunday in Advent — addresses the nature of the incarnation.*

There is an old story about a country church looking for its next pastor. The Chairperson of the Pastor Search Committee introduced a 17-year-old candidate and asked him, "Son, do you know the Bible pretty good?"

"Yes, sir," the young minister said, "pretty good. I know how Adam turned a serpent into a staff and used it to get water from a rock. I know how Moses and his family built a ship and sailed towards Tarshish. I know that Noah led the Israelites across the Dead Sea, walking on water. I know the story of Mary, how God promised her to one man who waited seven years to marry her only her sister got in line at the last minute and made her wait seven more years."

The Chairperson said to his committee, "I think we should call him as our pastor. He is young, but he sure knows his Bible."

We repeat some stories so often, know them so well, that if the details grow muddled we likely do not notice. The Christmas story, the birth narrative of Jesus, is like that. Last year I asked you how many wise men there were. You knew the answer, that we do not know the answer. The Bible does not say how many wise men there were. Likewise, no matter what our Christmas cards tell us, we are not certain what animals were in the manger, or what month Jesus was born, or how old Mary was.

So now let me throw you a real zinger, a genuine gotcha question: in what year was Christ born?

If you are thinking zero, or 1 AD, you are way off. Maybe you are thinking on or before 4 BC, because Herod, whom Matthew lists as King when Jesus was born, died on or before 4 BC. Therefore, Jesus had to have been born on or before 4 BC. And that is incorrect, also.

In what year was Christ born?

Christ was not born. If by Christ we mean the Messiah, the title used to describe the pledged arrival of God amidst humanity, the long-awaited fulfillment of God's covenantal promise to redeem human beings and the creation, if that is what we mean by Christ, Christ was not born. Christ has always been.

"In the beginning." These words ring a bell! They are the first words of the Bible. Genesis 1. "In the beginning, when God created the heavens and the earth ..."

These words also begin John's Gospel. Coincidence?

*"In the beginning was the Word, and the Word was with God, and the Word was God. He was in the beginning with God. All things came into being through him. Without him not one thing came into being."*

"In the beginning was the Word."

Who is this word? If by Christ we mean to name the part of God through which the world was made, who eventually took human flesh as a first century Jew named Jesus, we have to say that Christ was never born. Christ has always been. Christ is eternal. Christ is the Word.

We are about to engage some pretty heady stuff. Karl Barth said that "in the church of Jesus Christ there can and should be no non-theologians." This morning we shall scoot to the edge of our pews and engage our minds because we get to discuss that most delicious and curious of topics – the nature of God, the identity of God's word.

To understand the four canonical gospels, we must remember that they were written well after the events they report. Mark, Matthew, and Luke were written earlier than John, and scholars are not certain when John was written. Many believe that it may have been penned late as 90 or even 100 AD – a full generation or two after the resurrection. The questions simmering, then, within John's community were very different from the questions coming from Matthew, Mark, or Luke's communities.

Those first three gospels were interested with the details of the story. John is fascinated with the meaning of the story. "In the beginning was the Word." What is the word? We use the term so often: the Word of God. If I asked you to define "the word of God" – quickly now – you'd come up with three answers.

The Word is Christ. The Word is the Bible. The Word is the Bible preached and studied. [11]

John's Gospel teaches us that the Word is Christ. The Word is the second person of the Godhead. When we say in the Creed that we believe in God, "Father, Son, and Holy Spirit," the Word is the Son. The Word of God is the pre-existent – that means that Christ existed before Jesus was born – the pre-existent part of God which came bodily to be incarnated as Jesus. It is this Jesus whom we worship, and call Lord, and name Savior. It is this Jesus Christ – who lived, died, and was resurrected – in whom we discover the identity and purposes of almighty God. It is this Jesus which invites us into a vibrant and loving relationship with the eternal and living deity. This is what we mean when we use that term, the Word of God.

But we also mean the Bible. The Bible is the Word of God. The Bible is the written testament to God's covenant with God's people. The Bible tells the story of God's love for the world and for God's chosen image bearers upon it. The Bible records the details of that relationship, how God loved and blessed and disciplined and promised to send a Messiah to save and restore. The Bible is the written word which predicts, describes, and explains the Living Word – Jesus Christ. So this, also, is what we mean when we use that term, the Word of God.

But we also mean the Bible preached and studied. When we hear a sermon, or when we learn the Bible together, we allow ourselves to be touched again by the living Christ and the written testament to him – that he was promised, that he lived, died, and rose again, and that he will come again.

That also is what we mean by the Word: Jesus Christ, the Bible, the Bible preached and studied. All three.

Our challenge is remembering which is most important. The most important is Jesus Christ himself, and our experience of God made possible and personal through him. Our experience of God's love made evident and real through Jesus Christ, that is by far the most significant meaning of that very theological term, the Word of God.

Is it possible to take the Bible – a collection of written words about Jesus Christ – and read them, study them, dissect them, reduce

---

[11] See Shirley Guthrie, *Christian Doctrine: Revised Edition*, Westminster/John Knox Press, 1994, 62 ff.

them, magnify them – and grow nonetheless distant from the God they are meant to describe. Absolutely.

In Scotland they remember a telling story. Charles Wesley, one of the founders of Methodism, visited Scotland. In a valley sitting beneath a Church of Scotland parish church, he is said to have pointed to the church and quipped, "There the Word of God is turned back into word again." Word again. Only words. Mere words. Words can distract and belittle. Words can confuse and dismiss. Words can be quite *beside* the point. But the Word of God, the second person of the Godhead, the incarnate God/human being known as Jesus Christ, that Word *is* the point. Jesus Christ is that for which we have waited. Jesus Christ is the keeping of God's loving promises. Jesus Christ is the hope of all that is to come. The Word of God.

So, when John's Gospel was set to parchment those early Christians were clamoring for a deeper sense of what Jesus meant. If Jesus was God incarnate, so what? Why might that matter? John's Gospel was the answer, describing what God intended in Jesus.

I bet you have seen reports of that Christian billboard campaign. Graphically, the billboards are very simple: white letters on solid black backgrounds. They feature quotes attributed to God. One of my favorites is, "I do not question in your existence."

Another is quite revealing. "Do not make me come down there." Like a parent threatening the misbehaving children from atop the basement steps, God is imagined, hands on hips, "Do not make me come down there."

Some people imagine God that way. Threatening. Upset. Scolding. Irritated. Further, they cannot imagine that God would actually get involved. Holiness cannot enter the world without being tainted by the world, they suspect.

In John's day, people thought the same. Many suspected that Jesus was special, unique even, but not at his core, not ontologically, as the philosophers say. They believed that Jesus was an extraordinary human being, a prophet's prophet, so moral, so upright, so wise, that God chose him as a son. It was like God had adopted Jesus. God scanned human beings and said, "Finally, one of them got it right. I think I will make take him as a son." Theologians call this idea – not surprisingly – adoptionism. If Jesus was God's son, it was after the fact.

John's Gospel was written in part to say, No. That is not it. The Gospel, the good news, is actually much better than that. God came as God's very self. God did not send a human a surrogate. Not an adopted child. Not a substitute, a hired hand, an emissary, a messenger. God sent God's very self. Very God of Very God. Begotten, not made.

"In the beginning, when God created the heaven and the earth ..."

"In the beginning was the Word."

The Word, *that* Word, "became flesh and lived among us, and we have seen his glory, the glory as of a father's only son, full of grace and truth."

There is a funny little adage about breakfast: "The chicken has contributed. The pig is committed." Christmas is not about God's contribution to the world. Christmas is about God's commitment.

# Bulls, Bears, and Baptism

## Amos 8.1-12 and Mark 12.41-44

*This sermon was preached to students at Austin Presbyterian Theological Seminary in 2011. The stock market was only beginning to recovery amidst the worst recession since the 1930s. The Tea Party had been born. OccupyWallStreet was in the news.*

I am not much of a prophet if prognostication is a prerequisite. I am a terrible predictor. Last Thursday I went to bed early, certain that the Texas Rangers had the World Series Game 6 in the bag. Before that, in 2004, I actually believed that John Kerry was going to win the presidency.

But one prediction I nailed. I have been prophesying for five years that when more people understand the growing income gap, crowds will hit the streets.

Welcome to the Egyptian Spring, American style. OccupyWallStreet is how some have labeled the movement. The "99 percenters" is an alternative. Tent cities have sprouted in downtowns across the land. Their inhabitants have cobbled together a makeshift democracy and debate society. They elect leaders, appoint spokespersons, refine their message. The message is not very refined – and probably cannot be – as it erupts from angst too broad for bumper stickers. Its central impulse is that something is gravely wrong with our economic system and our leaders are not doing the right things to fix it.

What's curious is that the guitar strumming twenty somethings resemble – at least in their anger – the khaki clad middle agers who occupied the same parks only last spring. I speak, of course, of the Tea Party. Interestingly, the Tea Party is also possessed of the idea that something is gravely wrong with our economic system and our leaders are not doing the right things to fix it. Politics makes for strange bedfellows.

Here is how Slate Magazine contrasts the two movements. "Both are angry about what they see as economic unfairness – the Tea Party over deviations from free-market principle, the Occupiers over excessive adherence to it. Both are hostile toward society's elite, though they define that elite differently. Both are frustrated with the American political system." [12]

Newsflash. This just in from HuffingtonPost.com:

*"I am waiting to see what the religious response will be to OccupyWallStreet, which is a true revolution of the people. It is a cry from people who have been abused far too long by those who hold economic and political power. It is a cry for justice and compassion. ... What will the established churches say in response? Most likely, not very much ... When ministers speak out against systemic sin, they risk losing financial support. Congregants who benefit most from the economic status quo may leave and seek safer ground."* [13]

Now that is a prediction worth some thought.

A church member dropped by. He is a good man, a decent man. He announced that he was leaving the congregation. His wife, too. He read somewhere that the PC (USA) was recommending divestment from several companies doing business with Israel. Turns out, he owns that stock. I promise you that the church they joined will not mention divestment as a means to social justice.

Living in a declining empire, following Jesus in a society bearing its teeth and clinching its fists, practicing ministry with people enriched by but also diminished within an uneven economic system, what do we have to offer?

Much to the chagrin of the *Left Behind* crowd, Old Testament prophecy has a lot less to do with prediction than it does with proclamation. The prophets were inspired interpreters, keen observers. Prophets carried the word. They were word-bearers to God's people when God's people forget who and whose they were.

Amos certainly fit the bill. To a people content with summer fruit, he brought a message. People were hurting. While some grew fat, others grew gaunt. While some grew rich, more grew impatient. What was worse, God's people grew complicit. Amidst the injustice of it all, despite the unfairness, God's people did not speak. They did not act. In fact, they participated. In fact, they benefited. With deceit and false balances, they gamed the system. They could not wait for Sabbath to end so that they could get back to business.

---

[12] Jacob Weisbert, "Occupy Wall Street and the Tea Party: Compare and Contrast: One looks cooler. The other smells better. Do they agree on anything?, Slate.com, Oct. 13, 2011.

[13] Marilyn Sewell, "The Church and OccupyWallStreet," huffingtonpost.com, October 10, 2011.

When I told my dad that I wanted to be a minister, he said, "It will ruin your weekends."

Are you struck that words in their third millennia sound so contemporary? I know that Barth recommended a Bible for one hand and a newspaper for the other, but sometimes I wish I had longer arms. No wonder my Old Testament professor said that for the Hebrews, politics and religion were one and the same. Amos nails it. Amos describes our world, our context, us.

It seems almost sophomoric to observe something this obvious. Nonetheless, here it is. The market dynamics decried by the OccupyWallStreeters engulf us all. We are children of Wall Street. We benefit. Our pension fund depends on our investments. Our churches are funded by disciples who pledge based on their portfolios. Earnings on investments keep seminaries afloat, and denominations, and many congregations. The congregation I serve could not do half what it does without its endowment. The same economic devices which have shown 9% of the workplace to the door and put millions of homeowners underwater, those same economic devices pay our salaries and secure our futures. That is the simple truth.

Only it is not so simple. It is quite complex, practically and morally.

Are you uncomfortable yet? I am. The complexity of global capitalism and our interconnectedness with it can leave us paralyzed, stunned, slack jawed, silent. Years ago, somebody convinced me that Burger King contributes to deforestation in South America. Ranchers were clearing rain forests to create pastureland where Burger King's cows grew fat for slaughter. So, I quit buying Whoppers. That is simple, easy, and obvious.

But what are we to do in a world gone famously flat, where Chinese workers make cheap products we actually need, and for a pittance; a world where 40 percent of American college graduates move back in with their parents; a world where the best solution for insolvent banks is apparently to open the people's treasury to the very financiers who created this mess?

Amos nails it. "Shhhh. Hush. Now, listen up."

Then, into a conscience as only silence can prepare one, God spoke a harsh word. Into that silence God threatened … more silence. God promised a famine, but not of bread and water. God warned of a famine of "hearing the words of the Lord." It is as if

God said, "Since you will not listen to my words, I will no longer offer them" – the sacred silent treatment. No words, no relationship.

Could anything be worse? We are people of the Word. You are here to hear and to apply the Word to your lives. Amidst the injustice and the unfairness and the overwhelming complexity of it all, can you imagine anything worse than the impoverished silence of speaking to global capitalism without having the words of the Lord?

It was no idle threat. Frustrated at the complicity of God's people amidst economic unfairness, God surely was sorely tempted simply to shut up. Give them what they want. "Do what you damn well please," as my mother used to threaten.

Yet – and here is the good news – in the end, that is not who God is. God is WORD. God kept speaking. God gave words of hope and meaning to prophets and people alike, speaking always, calling passionately, pleading patiently. And when that did not do the trick God's Word took on flesh. God's Word dwelt among us, teaching the curious and touching the untouchable, feeding the hungry and challenging the complacent.

"Look at that widow," said the Word. "She lives on a fixed income, yet there she is, sharing it all." It is stewardship season. This text appears ever faithfully as an object lesson about proportionate giving and funding the institution, but it rarely makes the preacher's exegetical cut to observe Jesus' obvious condemnation that the widow was so poor in the first place.

So finally – and you know what it means when the preacher says finally; the women can put their shoes back on – finally, many of you are called to be preachers. Here you are learning to preach. Likely somebody has illustrated for you the importance of a sermon's ending, how, it you have got it right, there will be some last illustration or final story that will hang in people's minds, stick to people's guts. Rhetoricians recommend saving the best point for the last. And, if a sermon is about a gracious God, the last and best point is always one of grace. And hope. Preachers preach Gospel, and at the end, Gospel is always good news.

So where is the grace?

The hopeful lesson here is that God is finished with famines, finished with famines of the words of the Lord. God does not choose silence. The words of the Lord are still ringing true and sounding strong. The words of the Lord are decrying false weights and greedy measures. The words of the Lord condemn trampling on the needy and the bringing to ruin of the poor.

It just may be that the words of the Lord are not erupting from our sanctuaries but rather from our streets. That the church goes silent does not mean the Lord does. Is it possible that we do not so much go to the protesters with the word of the Lord so much as to hear it already there?

This preaching task is the spirited business of amplifying the words of the Lord above the cacophony of other words. But God's Word, it does not belong to us. It is a gift for us. When we muffle and mumble, the words of the Lord will find whispers and echoes in the most unexpected places.

Can we hear it? Will we amplify it?

So shhhh! Hush! Now, listen, you student preachers, for a Word from the Lord offered not through a monk, not through a mystic, not through a preacher, but through a minstrel, a songwriter. It is called *The Land of Plenty*, by Leonard Cohen.

> Do not really know who sent me
> To raise my voice and say:
> May the lights in The Land of Plenty
> Shine on the truth someday.
>
> For the millions in a prison,
> That wealth has set apart –
> For the Christ who has not risen,
> From the caverns of the heart –
>
>
> For the innermost decision,
> That we cannot but obey -
> For what's left of our religion,
> I lift my voice and pray:
> May the lights in The Land of Plenty
> Shine on the truth someday. [14]

---

[14] Leonard Cohen, "The Land of Plenty," on *Ten New Songs*, Sony Music, 2001.

# Do Not Be Afraid

## Matthew 28.1-10

*In my pastoral experience, many personal problems are rooted in fear. This sermon suggests that the Gospel is the best answer to it.*

What are you afraid of?

Likely you saw that question coming. With a sermon title like, "Do Not Be Afraid," it is the only place to start. What are you afraid of?

Now I do not mean what you might think I might. I am not talking about the kinds of fears tickled by Stephen King or Alfred Hitchcock or Edgar Allen Poe. Horror movies and psychological thrillers tell us something about ourselves, sure enough, but I am talking about something different.

I am also not asking you about your fears in the same way an evolutionary biologist would. I am not speaking about that internal switch within us that dictates fight or flight. I acknowledge that we are born with a natural fear of tigers and tarantulas, and it is fascinating to wonder how inherit fears from ancestors who lived closer to nature's dangers than we do. Likewise, it is an interesting question to study people's reactions when a burglar crawls through a window or we face an oncoming car on a one-way street. Be afraid. Fair enough. Still, that is not what I am talking about.

I am talking about something distinct. I am talking the kind of fears that often go unmentioned, often unnoticed. I am talking about the lingering voices of doubt which leave us anxious and lonely and unconfident.

And unless I miss my guess, you know what I am talking about. One person fears poverty, fears that there will not be enough. Someone fears that her husband loves her for the wrong reasons. Another fears being by himself and someone else fears going home to the emotional estrangement waiting there. I know people who feel incompetent and they fear the day they are discovered. (The imposter complex, they call it.) Someone else has a secret that he is desperately afraid will be discovered. Another has a secret She is desperately afraid will not be discovered. Sometimes we fear illness. Sometimes we fear change. Sometimes we fear things will stay the same. We fear we are not good enough. We fear we are not lovable enough. We fear that we will not have enough.

Our ultimate fear, in the end, is that such fears will accompany us to the very end. It was Woody Allen who quipped, "I am not afraid of death, I just do not want to be there when it happens."

We are complex and troubled beings. We are afraid of many things. As the bumper sticker has it, "If you are not afraid, you are not paying attention."

This morning's great good news is that God has something to say about this fear, something good, and something beautiful, and something true. God has a great deal to say about it, in fact! God says, "Do not be afraid."

Do not be afraid. My, but God is bossy. From time to time, God's instructions are crystal clear and quite uncompromising. The Bible is full of imperatives, too.

> "What does the Lord require of you but to do justice, and to love kindness, and to walk humbly with your God (Micah 6.8)?

> "You shall love the Lord your God with all your heart, and with all your soul, and with all your might" (Deuteronomy 6.5).

> Jesus offers the same.

> "But if anyone strikes you on the right cheek, turn the other also" (Matthew 5.39).

> "Love your enemies, do good, and lend, expecting nothing in return" (Luke 6.35).

> "If anyone forces you to go one mile, go also the second mile" (Matthew 5.41).

The Bible is full of imperatives. And of all these Biblical imperatives, "be not afraid" – or some similar sentiment – outnumbers all the rest. The same God who commands our worship and allegiance also directs us to release our fears. Do we allow God sufficient authority that we are willing to do so?

Some religious people allow God authority over their lives but in doing so, they inadvertently reduce religion to morality. Religion becomes the science of identifying and following rules, about segmenting reality and people into groups: people who follow the rules and those who do not, behavior which is right and behavior which is wrong, people like us and people who are like them!

Well, religion is not mere morality. Religion can be so much more. Religion can be a vibrant love affair with God.

Can we love such a bossy God? Repent! Judge not! Forgive seven times seventy!

So this morning, we awaken in a graveyard. It is Easter morning, the central moment in the history of the species. Jesus is dead and those who love him have come to the tomb. We know the story – all three versions – because we have followed the ritually righteous to church every springtime of our lives to hear it retold. This August Sunday morning – half a year's remove from Easter lilies and ham – we might see the story through new eyes, however.

Because what is happening in the graveyard is not only that Jesus was dead and now he is not. What is happening in this is this; God is disclosing that God is not what people had made him out to be.

People were afraid of God. They always had been. God was feared, always feared. God was angry and jealous and ready to smite, always ready to smite somebody. Anybody. Maybe one's enemies. Maybe even God's chosen. So to approach God required sacrifice. That is what it meant to be God-fearing. When you approach God, tread lightly. God is angry. Demanding. On the edge. Ready to snap.

That immature understanding of God was near universal. It is why primitive peoples threw virgins off cliffs. It is why our spiritual ancestors streamed to Jerusalem to sacrifice the fatted calf, the finest lamb. All of it assumed that God was on the edge of temper and that we were standing on the last nerve. Only by giving up the best might God's people appease God's anger. God was, God is, to be feared.

God was mighty, powerful, regal, and angry. God was omniscient, omnipotent, omnipresent, and angry. God was demanding, hard driving, perfectionistic, and angry.

So any relationship with God began with – you guessed it – fear.

Which goes to our deepest fear, of course, because whether we are afraid that our spouse does not really love us or that we will outlive our money – no matter our fear –all fear is at root about our lack of control. Fear is the emotional acknowledgment that we are not in control. Fear, you might even say, is the frantic pain of not being God. Fear stems from our not being God.

If that is true, that fear stems from our not being in control, our not being God, and if God is understood as someone to be afraid of, well, we can begin to see the enormity of God's task. How could God possibly convince us that God is not to be feared, and rather to be loved? God kept saying it, time and time again, from the Bible's earliest pages. You have heard mere snippets this morning, the briefest litany of God saying over and over, "Do not be afraid. Do not be afraid. I am in control. It will be all right. Do not be afraid. That litany reached its crescendo in a first century graveyard when Mary and Mary hear it yet again, singing distance from an empty tomb, "Do not be afraid."

If you really think the world a fearsome place, that death and anxiety and fear will have the final say, God says, "Let me show you different. I will come and be with you. I will be one as you. I will be a human being, and I will rise victorious from everything you think is final, from pain, from estrangement, from sin, from death itself. I will show you that you have nothing to fear by defeating everything that you fear."

What if God really means it? What if God is completely authentic in commanding us not to fear? What if God actually is in control, and what if God really does love us through and through, and what if God really can be trusted? If all this is true – that God is the Lord of the Universe, and that God is love, and that God is steadfast and trustworthy – what, then, is there to fear?

# The Resurrection Body

## Luke 24:36b – 49

*Most Protestant Mainliners do not clamor for doctrinal sermons.*
*This does not mean that we should not preach them.*

I noticed a teaser for a radio program about what happens to us when we die. Nationally syndicated RadioLab enticed listeners to tune in with questions like, "Does the soul have weight?" and "Can the dead play tennis?" Answering such questions seems a tall order for a weekly radio show. People have been asking such questions since there have been people to ask questions.

The disciples were wondering, too. Just recount the journey of discovery they have led us on for these last two weeks.

Mary discovers the empty tomb. Peter and the other disciple verify its emptiness. Then, the gardener – AKA the risen Jesus – meets Mary in the garden. That was Easter's story, two Sundays ago.

Last Sunday the disciples invited us into their story on the evening of that first Easter. They are in an upper room, trembling behind locked doors. The risen Jesus appears and offers them peace. Thomas is not there, though, and he vows never to believe unless he touches "the mark of the nail in [Jesus's] hands," pledges never to believe until he puts his hand "in Jesus's side." Thomas, it turns out, is a tactile kind of guy. Seeing will not be enough. Touching will be required.

So, a week later Jesus appears again to the remaining eleven disciples and for all his threats and requirements Thomas nonetheless confesses the risen Jesus his "Lord" and his "God" upon sight alone.

Now this contest between seeing and touching is a big deal in the first century. Jews in Jesus's day were divided on whether there is any resurrection at all. For those who believed in resurrection, it was not to an instant one, something that happens when we die. The resurrection would occur on "the last judgement," someday, off in the future. So, like some very early RadioLab, there was all sorts of speculation about where people went to wait, and whether they were awake in the meantime.

Now, on this third Sunday of Easter, we leap from John's Gospel to Luke's and the risen Jesus has come again. Once more, he greets his disciples with peace. This is yet one more way of God saying, "Do not be afraid. I am here, with you."

No matter how peacefully Jesus has shown up, the disciples are "startled and terrified." Why? They think they are seeing a ghost. So Jesus calms his disciples. How? He assures them that he is not a ghost. He invites them to touch his body. Then – catch this – he eats a piece of fish. Ghosts do not eat – sardines, salad, or spaghetti. Ghost do not eat.

What is going on here? Well, it is complicated. It was complicated twenty centuries ago and it is even more complicated now.

Next, Jesus was comforting his frightened disciples with at least three world changing promises.

First, in Jesus, God had defeated human death by actually dying one. He really was dead, and then, he really was not.

Second, Jesus makes no promises that he will not keep. When he tells his disciples that he is going ahead to prepare a place for them, Jesus is saying to people of flesh and blood that their afterlife will be prefaced because of his. In other words, the risen Christ is flesh and blood because unless Jesus' flesh and blood are taken into heaven to prepare a place for us, we can never follow.

To first century Jews who believe, if they believe in resurrection at all, that it will occur someday, in the far future, an immediate afterlife as something other than as disembodied spirits was an idea to behold, indeed.

Our spiritual ancestors continued to wonder what it all meant. In the first four centuries the early church continued to wrestle with these promises and with these early firsthand reports.

Some decided that Jesus had been God, alright, but not human. Bunk, the early church concluded. Read the firsthand reports. Jesus was human. Even after his death he invited the disciples to touch his skin and he ate fish with them. Whatever else may be said about Jesus of Nazareth, he was fully human. How else, the early church asked, could God redeem the entire created order? The risen Christ is flesh and blood because the created world of molecules and molehills and trees and skin can be redeemed only by one who is made of the same stuff.

I admit the sheer folly of summarizing two millennia of thought on the nature of Jesus' resurrection body in a 15-minute sermon. Well, okay, a 17-minute sermon. But still, let us rush ahead.

Perhaps you are aware that most of us were born into a world emerging from something called modernism. The modern world thought science was neat and tidy, confident and complete. Modernity believed that science could explain all our questions and define most of our world. The thinking went that if we stick with the methods of science, human knowledge will someday run across a complete understanding of curing cancer and space travel and how the universe works. The entire universe, the argument went, is governed by a set of immutable laws, discoverable laws, and they await our discovery.

So, the modernists argued, we have no evidence that dead people get up and walk around and pass through walls and eat fish, except for the Bible, of course, so something must give. And those modernists who were Christian were not ready to throw out the stories of the Bible, so they sought interpretive tools to synthesize the Bible with science. Faith and reason can exist side by side. Science and religion are friends, not foes. The Bible tells us who and why. Science tells us how and when. We can take the Bible seriously but not literally. And, we can take science literally without compromising our religious faith. God created the universe over 13.8 billion years. God nudged evolution towards homo sapiens around 200,000 years ago. Evolution is a tool of God's providence.

You get the idea.

And Jesus rose physically, flesh and blood, from the dead? It is a metaphor, some said. It is a myth, others argued, but only in the best sense of that term. Jesus did rise again, you see, if in the hearts and minds of his followers. Jesus lives, the argument went, if you allow him to live in your heart.

Now I do not mean to be hard on the modernists. The bodily resurrection is, no doubt, quite something to swallow. The Apostle Paul could not explain it, at least not very well. He tried, you know. Paul tried to explain what happens in resurrection and ended up saying that we do have bodies after death, like Jesus's body. They are not the same bodies we have now, of course. Rather, they are something called "spiritual bodies."

Spiritual bodies. And perhaps you are like a good many other people who find that helpful, but rather incomplete. Would you not like a more detailed explanation for what life after death will be, a more scientific explanation? Modernism explained away or nervously neglected the bodily resurrection as incompatible with our understanding of the world. So many faithful Christians had to think of new ways to understand what it meant that Jesus was dead and then he was not.

Then a funny thing happened on the way to the laboratory. Modernity dissipated. If you did not know it, we live now in something called the Post-Modern Age. Post modernism is not exactly a rejection of modernism. Rather, it questions modernism's confidence in the ability of science alone to understand the world. There is stuff we cannot know, postmodernism argues. In fact, science itself has demonstrated that there is stuff we just cannot figure out.

Take Einstein, who teaches us that space and time are relative. Quantum physics now shows us that the universe has to include uncertainty (we can never know both the position and velocity of sub-atomic particles), and paradox (electrons appear as both particles and waves), and chaos (an observable randomness in physical causation that remains mysterious.) Now you may not understand what I just said. I do not.

But I do understand that this postmodern world is bringing humility to spiritual matters, and that the arrogant intellectual bravado of modernity is in some ways passing away. Postmodernity is giving thinking Christians some thinking space within which to ask again what it means that Jesus rose from the dead.

And believe it or not, this matters in how we live our lives.

It all has to do with the fusion of, and the balance between, the soul and the body. If Jesus rose from the dead, you see, our souls, and our bodies, are in some deeply mysterious way so intertwined that they cannot be pulled apart.

You are a body. You are a soul. At the same time. And should by the grace of God any of us should survive death, the same will be true on the other side.

And why does this matter?

If the drive-through line at Starbucks is twelve cars deep, do you park your car and go inside, or do you continue to flood the air with exhaust that contributes to global climate change?

If the human Jesus rose from the dead, you will be concerned about the created world he died to redeem.

You are a body. You are a soul. At the same time. And should by the grace of God any of us should survive death, the same will be true on the other side.

And why does this matter?

It means that hospitals still give free parking to ministers. If you go into the hospital, do you want to see your doctor only, or will you welcome a visit from your pastor, too? Is healing your body the only goal, or is it somehow interwoven with tending your soul as well?

If the human Jesus rose from the dead, you will want both.

You are a body. You are a soul. At the same time. And should by the grace of God any of us should survive death, the same will be true on the other side.

And why does this matter?

If the doctor hands you a test result which is the equivalent of a death sentence, what will you do with the rest of life? Will you hurry to the finish line, or will you live every moment with every ounce of energy your body and soul can contribute?

Kate Bowler is an Assistant Professor at Duke Divinity School. A young thirtysomething, she is married to her high school sweetheart. They have a little boy. Not too long ago Kate was diagnosed with cancer. She is currently in remission. She has written a little book called *Everything Happens for a Reason and Other Lies I Have Loved*.

She describes coming across a newspaper article summarizing interviews with people who have had near death experiences. The authors interviewed people with all kinds of experiences, all variety of knocking at death's door. Many of them, it turns out, experience the same feeling: love. The article struck Dr. Bowler, so very sophisticated with a PhD and teaching experience and scholarly respectability. She writes,

> *"I am sure I would have ignored the article if it had not reminded me of something that happened to me, something that I felt uncomfortable telling anyone. It seemed too odd and too simplistic to say that I knew to be true – that when I was sure I was going to die, I did not feel angry. I felt loved."* [15]

---

[15] Kate Bowler, *Everything Happens for a Reason and Other Lies I have Loved* (New York: Random House 2018), 120-121.

Bowler felt loved.

I have now endured two surgeries with awful morbidity rates and long survival odds. And of all that I felt, love was the most important, the most enveloping, the most enduring. Love. "And now faith, hope, and love abide, these three; and the greatest of these is love" (1 Corinthians 13.13).

What was the nature of Christ's resurrection body? He was not a ghost. He ate fish and he walked through locked doors. There is something quite mysterious and unexplainable about it all.

But of this we are certain. Our uncertainty finds its peace in the presence of divine love. One who shares our very nature has taken it deep into the very heart of God. And this changes how we will live, this side of death, and the other.

# When Towers Stand Forever

## Proverbs 18.10

"The name of the Lord is a strong tower;
The righteous run into it and are safe."

*On Tuesday, September 11, 2001, terrorists attacked the
World Trade Centers, the Pentagon, and crashed a crowded
airliner into a Pennsylvania field. Sometimes, prose falls short. I
preached this sermon the following Sunday. It seemed clear to me,
even then, that the events would be used as a pretext for a middle
east war.*

United we stand,
if stunned,
you and I,
connected now by untended bonds
on a Manhattan street
ankle-deep in modern dust:
other people's financial statements
strewn about
with yesterday's hopes and delusions.

Madness.
Our former lives punctured by Boeings
crumbling downward, inward
countrymen, women descending stairwells
up, too, with fire hats and bravery
heroes/victims
time stood still
how many days already?
Five.
Time does not fly when ashes linger.

Astronauts spied this carnage from on high
while we transfixed
by the uncouth glow of television screens
sat simultaneously unscathed
except our personal perceptions
vandalized by reporters' commentary.

Yet from perches higher still
One watches.
One, before memory began,
One, before
Eden's planting
floods receding
Sarah laughing
Abraham promising
Hebrews running
prophets howling
three religions birthing
all to make a point:
nothing stops love.
*We believe.*

So ankle-deep in questions and turmoil
we collect ourselves and our memories
scripture snippets colliding.
"Thou shalt not kill."
"Seven times seventy."
"Turn the other cheek."
"An eye for an eye."
Who was it who said,
"Vengeance is mine"?
"Blessed are the peacemakers,
for they shall inherit the earth."

But God, what kind of earth shall we bequeath?
Our land of liberty-gone-awry
welcomes some whose heaven-door
   must be bombed open.
Strange:
chest thumping believers
macho-young-men
bodies formed but spirits, not.
Women and widows do not hijack.
Religion's right
turned into false confidence
   laying blame not love.

Shall we watch meekly by as
delusion parades as honor
   muscle masks as morality?
What of orphan and widow
defenseless all;
   do we stand, or run?
O God,
sackcloth and ashes
won't do it this time.

Thus, we come where always we go
when yesterday and tomorrow
seem disconnected.
Ashes to ashes, dust to dust
we shall return to You
even
especially
   now.
We need not die
for you our strength and protector to be.
Thank God. Thank you, God.

So here we are.

Thank you, God
for acts of bravery and selflessness
known only to you
if not the *Today Show*.
Thank you, God
for receiving thousands crumbling down
now buoyed up.
Thank you, God
for children held and
parents phoned
and family ties now double knotted.
Thank you, God
for identities reclaimed and
allegiances recommitted.

Thank you, God
for nations turned together
not away.
Thank you, God
for Moslem friend, and Jew
speaking love not hate.
Thank you, God
for reaching out
when we turn in.
Thank you, God
for your regular busyness
of bringing
light from dark
rising from falling
resurrection from death.
Thank you, God
for crying
with us
for in your tears
we founder to islands of hope.

So now we faraway stare
to future unclear, dusty still
and we remember
who we are
where we have been
to whom we belong.

We celebrate and trust
that any God who did it once
and more
will do it again:
unite us *for* the world
not *against* it;
guide us forward;
keep us faithful;
show us how you selfless
mend this broken world.

And when it is done,
O God of Peace,
hold us still and
forgive us
for no victor will Abraham's tears dry.
When might has not made right
but merely destruction tempered,
draw our eye to distant hope where
someday
towers stand forever.

God bless America.
God bless the faithful everywhere,
  today, tomorrow, and always.

# Bosnia and Babylon

## Ezekiel 37:1-14

*This sermon was preached in Lent, 1996, following the revelation of war crimes committed against Moslem communities in the Bosnian War.*

We stand, you and I,
  in a valley of dry bones
  surrounded by the filthy fibulas of foot soldiers
  in the far-away battlefield
  which is not Ezekiel's valley
but something like it.

True, we are not Judah.
  We are not scattered in Babylonian exile.
  Our culture has not been dissolved.
  Our temple has not been destroyed.
  Our congregation has not been scattered.
  Our will to worship has not been snuffed
      though many are hearing echoes.
Maybe they are right.

Friday's newscast bragged.
  Garrick Utley has a scoop.
  Stories of mass murder outside Srebrenica are true. [16]
    Madeline Albright has never been so close to human remains
    eight thousand maybe
    Moslems
    slaughtered by Christians
  buried by frantic bulldozers
  caught in the act
  by cameras miles in the sky
brought to my living room by the seedy miracle of television.

---

[16] ABC News, broadcast March 22, 1996.

I stand in that Bosnian valley
   and you do too
   with Madeline Albright
   and Ezekiel.


      *"Our bones are dried up,*
      *and our hope is lost;*
      *we are cut off completely."*


Ash Wednesday ushered us to Lent.
     "Remember that you are dust and to dust you will return."
Harsh words
   uncomfortable to hear.
God is God.
We are not God
   in the valley of dry bones
2600 years ago
or Friday.


      *"Our bones are dried up,*
      *and our hope is lost;*
      *we are cut off completely."*


Of course we stand neither in Babylon or Bosnia.
So why not turn our heads
   close our eyes
   change the channel?
We cheer not in battles between
   Babylonians and Judahites
   Serbs and Croats.
To care about such far flung conflicts
   confuses us
Why?
Why, God?
Why care?


Because like Ezekiel's,
   our battlefield soon becomes a graveyard
   where lie the bones
   of little girls who jumped rope

old women who wrote poetry
men who shaved before plodding off to work
Granddad and Uncle John and Sister Sally.
The battle slays not just the soldier
  but whole peoples
  hope
  our will to worship God.

Our battles are different from Ezekiel's battles
  unlike the struggles of Srebrenica's widows
  yet we each have tragedies
  broken dreams
  rotting relationships
  deaths un-mourned
  walls
separating us from God
  hope
  worship.

To deny Bosnian battles
  is to reject our own
  and to deny our own battles
is to exile God.

So we fall on bended knee
  and plead with God
  that walls will tumble into obscurity
  flowers will grow in graveyards
bones will rise and breathe again.

> *The Lord said to me, "Mortal,*
> *can these bones live?"*
> *I answered, "O Lord God, you know."*

Ezekiel challenges us,
  "Do not change the channel
  or turn your eye
    for when you do
  you silence your pleading.
  To banish God from Srebrenica
is to banish God from here.

If God is God
   in valleys of dry bones
   we may trust
   that there is a reason
   God desires us
   to stand in unclean ruins
of sin gone wild.

For hope breathes
   not in shallow gusts of mere optimism
   but in the sustaining breeze of
      wind
      breath
      Spirit
   which billowed Adam's lungs in Eden's garden
     and hovered within Ezekiel's vision
    above moving, living hordes of an Israel reborn.

Spirit
   sustains me
   and you
   within the dust
of human life.

The staggering news
   that we are God's
   is nothing less than the stunning Word
   that God empowers
   bones to breathe
   fractures to heal
love to win.

So we do not change the channel
   or avert our eyes
   or live behind tragedy's walls
   precisely
   because
   God is God
in the valleys of our dry bones.

Praise be to God!
Praise be to God!

In joyous worship
  bone is given marrow.
On bended knee
  we drip with life.
From our place
  this time
  we erupt
  side by side
  boney hands clasped left and right
  walking in lines
  with breathy joy
  through the valley
  collecting the wounded
  the dying
  the bones
for Christ.

# Forgive me, Jerry, for I Have Sinned

## Matthew 6:1-6, 16-21, 2 Corinthians 5:20b-6:10, and Isaiah 58:1-12

*Referencing Jerry Springer and similar television shows in this Ash Wednesday 1998 sermon, I observed to the congregation that "we are not much like Jerry's guests." Among that evening's congregation was a woman who admitted, on her way out of the sanctuary, that she and her daughter had appeared on the Sally Jesse Raphael Show. Lesson learned.*

Confessing sin is an inborn human need, and I want to offer this as proof: television talk shows.

TV talk shows range from bizarre to funny, from sickening to just plain weird. Out of curiosity I checked Jerry Springer's homepage on the internet to see which carnivals he hosted last week. Consider his offerings. Remember, I am not making these up!

""Honey, I am a call girl," in which a man pleads with his girlfriend to leave prostitution while her pimp looks on."

""I'll Never Let You Go!" in which Taiwana furiously confronts her fiancé, Chrishon, because he is living with another woman, even though they will marry in three weeks."

Jerry Springer is not alone, of course. Jenny Jones has recently celebrated her 1000th episode with offerings like this one: "My Teen's Body Is Getting Curves, But Her Attitude's Getting on My Nerves!"

Throw in Ricki Lake, Geraldo Rivera, Maury Povich, Sally Jesse Raphael, and even on occasion the less sensational Oprah Winfrey, and you have a full-fledged phenomenon. This is more than show business. It is big business. A sizable chunk of America's population clearly has some shared, inner need to bathe in the public airing of grievances, dirty laundry, and tawdry escapades.

Do you know many people in these sorts of ... well, unconventional situations? These television shows seek the most sensational, eccentric, fantastic stories they can find. Many of these folks are in situations which are just plain bizarre.

What in the world do we have in common with them?

Here is what; people have a built in need to confess. We bear an instinct to admit our personal brokenness. When we hurt others, we feel bad. When we diminish ourselves by immoral behavior, we feel guilty. When we neglect deeds that will build a better world, and better relationships, we sense a missed opportunity. Most people know when we need to confess, even if we do not call it confessing. It is called a conscience. God installed it.

My daughter just turned three years. Madelene was in the nursery last Wednesday during children's church school. They rushed her to me in the Fellowship Hall. She was sobbing. She clung to me tight, saying over and over again, "I am sorry. I am sorry." I asked what had caused this first ever outburst of remorse. It seems that some ten minutes before Madelene had pushed a baby swing into Hannah, another kid in the nursery. Hannah had cried, but she had gotten over it quickly. Madelene had not. Ten minutes later, here she was, still crying, repeating, "I am sorry. I am sorry."

I thought about that for a long time. Maybe Madelene had meant to hurt Hannah. Perhaps she had learned the ugly human truth that it is within each of us to hurt others. Maybe Maddie's tears were tears of guilt. Or maybe she had not meant to hurt Hannah at all. It had just simply happened. Perhaps she had simply learned the hard lesson that we live in a world where we hurt others even when we do not mean to. It is an equally difficult lesson. Maybe her tears were tears of empathy.

We will never know if her tears were tears of guilt or of empathy. I am certain that we learned something about Maddie that day; she has both a heart and a conscience.

Most human beings have – deep down, hard wired, permanently installed – a need to confess our sin. Could that be why a prostitute will tell the man she loves that she has betrayed him, even if it means doing so on a national broadcast? Is that why people reveal their deepest secrets over the airwaves, for the first time and often to unsuspecting loved ones?

Television talk shows simply provide an inappropriate way to confess sin for people who seek no better venue.

So let us talk about Ash Wednesday. Ash Wednesday begins the liturgical season of Lent and as such provides our first step in a journey towards Easter. Lent is the forty days leading up to Easter Sunday, not counting Sundays. You will remember that forty is an important number in the Bible. It rained forty days and forty nights on Noah's Ark. Moses and the Israelites wandered forty years in the desert before entering the Promised Land. Jesus outlasted forty days of temptation before beginning his ministry.

Lent lasts forty days. Each of these stories – Noah, Moses, and Jesus' temptation – have a common theme. God calls a leader to reconcile God's people to God. God people wander, but despite it all, God calls God's people back. From the flood, God brings new life. From Egyptian slavery, God brings forth a people.

From Jesus's faithfulness, God brings eternal forgiveness and reconciliation.

That is the word, is not it? Reconciliation. People wander. God calls us back, calls us back so that we might be reconciled with God. Reconciled with one another. So each Ash Wednesday we remember the wondrous promise of eternal reconciliation.

And it begins with confession. That is why the prostitute confesses the truth to her boyfriend; in the hope that they can be reconciled. That is why the fiancé asks her boyfriend for a confession; in the hope of reconciliation. That is why Jesus let them execute him rather than walk away and die an old man in his sleep. God knew that reconciliation was impossible without confession, and to confess is to see ourselves honestly, truthfully. We are creatures capable of great beauty and grace and promise, but also of great evil. As Frederick Buechner has observed, perhaps each of us is "six parts chicken, phony, slob."

The Scottish poet Robert Burns touched on the divine when he noted this:

> *Oh wad some power the giftie gie us*
> *To see oursel's as others see us!*

For those of us who do not speak Scots, I had to look up the translation:

> *Oh, what some power the gift God gave us*
> *To see ourselves as others see us!*

Ash Wednesday is God's gift, to see ourselves as God sees us. God sees us through the loving eyes of one who would have died for you if you had been the only one.

Now, before whom would you rather confess: Jerry Springer, or God?

Each of tonight's three readings point to what our lives should look like this Lenten season. Isaiah decries Israel's false religious practices. It points to people who talk the talk but do not walk the walk. It speaks of people who go through the public ritual of religion but remain unchanged. Likewise, Paul warns us not to receive grace in vain. God's forgiveness leads to something – our transformation. To confess, and to receive forgiveness, is to commit oneself to authentic change. Finally, Jesus reminds us of the essential interiority of the religious life. It is a terribly personal thing, our relationship with God. It is personal, but it is never private. We are to live our lives as transformed, forgiven people.

I have another daughter, an older daughter. She turns five in a couple of weeks. She is an amazing little person. She is learning to be sneaky. She has a good idea of what her parents think is right, and what is wrong. She avoids doing what we think is wrong, at least when we are around.

From time to time the house will get strangely quiet. Now Audrey is a rambunctious, active five-year-old. When things are quiet, she is either asleep, or she is up to something. In the middle of the day, you can bet she is not asleep. So, when things are quiet, and I know she is in her bedroom, I will shout, "Audrey, where are you?"

I know very well where she is. She is in her bedroom. I am not actually asking her where she is. I am calling her to accountability because I know what she is capable of – both bad and good. I am reminding her that if she is up to mischief, I care enough to notice.

Ash Wednesday is God's calling, calling out to us where we are. "Where are you? Where are you in your lives? Are you in a faithful place, or is your heart looking elsewhere? Are you striving for Christian faithfulness, or are you chasing other, false gods?"

I do not know where you are tonight. I struggle to define where I am. But I do know that Lent is the time to find the answer. Whichever sin might be leading us away, whatever alienation may be keeping us from reconciliation, whatever regret or deed undone, I know that tonight we may carry it to this table and leave it here.

The worship service which began with the ashes of death leads us now to the bread of life. Here is the Lord's Table, where bad blood is transfused with good. With Christ's blood. The new covenant.

Come. Taste. See that the Lord is good.

# Life at Younger Field
## Genesis 3:1-7 and Colossians 1:11-20

*In this day when "thus sayeth the Lord" must rival "it seems to me" in the pulpit, autobiography can be an acceptable entrance into Biblical and theological conversation. This sermon attempts to access a deeper matter through a regional obsession: football.*

I aged a lifetime one cold Friday night on Younger Field. What at evening's start was a colorful garden became at night's end a desert wasteland.

Younger Field is the football stadium in my hometown. Like hundreds of small-town stadiums, Younger Field becomes in the fall the center of the community and its battles animate coffee shop conversations the rest of the year. They call it Monday Morning Quarterbacking, but it continues on Tuesdays, too, and in December, and in March, endless discussions about who did what, and, Are any of our upcoming sophomores any good? Over tables at Heard and Jones Drugstore and Vaughn's Coffee Shop and the aptly named Hornet Restaurant, the town found in football a language to span its barriers.

Friday night football. The marching band's brass section – from tubas to French horns – plays *On Wisconsin* until their lips throb and their mouthpieces freeze in the winter wind. Young women actually compete for the right to don short skirts and jump endlessly in thunderstorms and snow flurries. Booster Club parents sell Frito pie and hot cocoa to raise money for the program. "We might need the extra money to pay for the team's transportation. Maybe we will go to the playoffs this year."

The town reminded us football players that the game of football is somehow like the rest of life, only more so. And because life's day-to-day challenges are acceptably amplified on the field, the town's encouragement allowed a language unacceptable in any other forum: hit 'em again, hit 'em again, *harder, harder*; push 'em back, *push* 'em back, way back; get that ball and really *fight*!

All of this takes enormous preparation. Practice. Foresight. Planning. The band marches 5 days a week, 2 hours a day. The Booster Club meets each Tuesday nights to review last week's game film with the coaching staff, and to get the inside story and the scouting report on the coming Friday's game plan. The cheerleaders practice every afternoon, hopefully near enough to the football team that both they and the players can catch the occasional and surreptitious glimpse of the other. And the football team practices endlessly. How I remember those practices: fingers jammed and swollen, grass burns and Band Aids fused together in a natural if nauseating marriage of young masculine bravado, endless drills with names none of us could explain, but once we could say them, and do them, we too were now in a secret fraternity and it did not matter what they meant: gomers, belly-ups, carioca, and monkey rolls.

What mattered was that we were now in the fraternity, in the group, in the *community*. No matter what those Whirlwinds and Bobcats and Antelopes could throw at us, we had each other. We were Hornets. (If you do not understand the dynamics of modern teen gangs, take a look at high school athletics.) And those football practices, those long, tedious, painful practices, they forged us into a team. The coaches would glare and gloat until we got it right. Their whistles blew, and their voices howled and somehow through the violence of it all we came together – despite ourselves, and despite last week's thrashing!

You see, this is what I mean about the innocence of Younger Field. We mounted the stage each week with confidence and clean uniforms, knowing that tonight was all that mattered. Win or lose, there was always another chance. There would always be next Friday night, or even better, next season. Our coaches could always reinstill a blind confidence that we were good, that last week did not really matter, that if we worked hard and cared, only good things would come. The future held no power because the present held no consequence. Win or lose, we could still play the game. There is an essential innocence to this competition, with no consequence except bragging rights until next year. The Super Bowl is not super at all, not compared to this. These young participants do these things out of *love*. They play this game of music and hoopla and combat out of an innocent fascination, a wonderfully naive metaphor about life and love, power and war.

I wonder if Mr. Younger knew what an honest description his name would lend to this particular field of combat. Younger Field.

I can no longer play there. Mostly this is due to an aging body and a frail, abandoned spirit of competition. But the real reason I can no longer play on Younger Field is that only the young can play on such a field. Only the innocent.

I left my innocence on Younger Field on an October night a lifetime ago. The Wildcats had made their biannual visit to do battle with the hometown Hornets. The Wildcats versus the Hornets -- sounds like a perfectly natural Garden variety brawl, does it not? This was to be my next-to-last high school football game, when I would still be on the team, on the field. More important, it was to be my last game in the hometown stadium. My family was to move away in less than a month. I was about to grow up.

I do not honestly remember if we won or lost that football game. As always fans filled the stands and my nerves were on end and the band played each time we crossed the goal line. At half-time the coaches gave us the same speech we always got, the door-slamming mad man routine designed to make us feel we were letting ourselves down, and our parents, our school, indeed our entire town. (If you think guilt is used as a motivator in church, visit any high school football locker room.)

In the third quarter our offense had the ball on our own 40-yard line. Coach called "Killer 7 base." As I had done a hundred times, I took the fullback stagger-step left and headed for the seven hole. The quarterback planted the ball in my belly. I followed the tight end's trap block, planted left and cut right, and spotted the rover coming from the flat. Doing just as I had been taught to do – coached to do, *programmed* to do – I cradled the ball, dipped my head down and hit the rover head-on. He fell. I stepped over him as I ran on. The safety tackled me some yards down the field.

Instinctively I handed the ball to the referee and headed home to the Hornet huddle. On the way, however, I noticed that a couple of wayward Wildcats had gathered around their teammate. He was not getting up. His teammates swarmed him in concern. My teammates noticed. Some patted my behind in this only place where that is accepted, and said, "Good hit, Travis! Good hit! You really took him down."

The opposing coach sprinted onto the field, and I watched, five yards off. "Move your legs, son," he pleaded.

"Coach, I cannot. I cannot move my legs. I cannot move my arms, either."

My coach came out on the field, too, to do what he could. He could do nothing. No one could. They hailed the ambulance.

I cried the tears of Adam and Eve as they hoisted that Wildcat into the ambulance. The water of salt dripped down my cheeks. No face mask could hide it. I was profoundly confused. Part of me was pleased to have hit someone so hard, to have shown someone who was who, to have exercised such devastating power over another. But another part of me, the better part, saw the pain of what I had done. And I felt ashamed, ashamed of feeling even an ounce of glee.

My teammates did not understand. My tears baffled them. After all, I had merely done was what we had all been coached to do. Why was I upset? None knew what to say or do.

Except Jim. Jim was the sole teammate to wrap his arms around me and tell me that it was okay, that this football player would be all right. On that cold Friday night, so many years ago, with tears wetting my cheek, a teammate held me and told me that it would be all right.

I cannot remember the rest of the game. After it, when I had taken off my football gear I noticed my dad in the locker room. Unlike that television commercial where the father hands the defeated son a Lifesaver, it was clear to us both that no Lifesaver would do it this time. I think, looking back, that my dad was at his best at that moment, at his most instinctive, his most compassionate. He said, "Let's go to the hospital." He knew. He knew!

I did not shower. We went straight to Swisher Memorial Hospital. We found the young man in the back of the ambulance, soon to be taken to a larger hospital where maybe they could help. I reached into the ambulance and I said to him, "I am sorry. I am so sorry." He either did not hear me, or he chose not to talk to me. To this day I do not know which. I know only that decades later the memory of that moment burns still, that in that lack of exchange I learned something about human life that no marching band, no squad of cheerleaders, can speak to.

Adam and Eve ate of the tree of knowledge. Having eaten, they looked up, and their eyes "were opened, and they knew that they were naked; and they sewed fig leaves together and made loincloths for themselves."

We call this the Fall. It is pedestrian to observe that we human beings live in world marked by failure and disobedience and sin. So deeper still, we acknowledge that that each of us is marked by sin and disobedience. No, we are not evil to the core. Sin does not rule our every thought, govern our every moment. We do not sin every time, or all the time.

The story of Eve and Adam's fall reminds us of the mournful truth that we live our stories in a world in which, even if we were perfect – and we are not – still, we cannot escape the sin of others. The Fall is a way to describe our essential situation, living life and seeking love from a posture of imperfection.

We live in a fallen world. What I learned on Younger Field is that we can follow the rules, we can fairly apply the techniques of the game, we can please the crowd and maybe even they'll play *On Wisconsin* for you, but still, we hurt people. And we get hurt. Because the rules are not perfect, and the field is never completely level, and we human beings are constantly changing our minds about who we are rooting for.

But there is good news. One has come who understands the rules of our game. In him we may withstand its limitations. As Colossians has it, "He has rescued us from the power of darkness and transferred us into the kingdom of his beloved Son, in whom we have redemption, the forgiveness of sins." While all may not yet be well, it is going to be.

In the meantime, God promises the forgiveness of Jesus Christ, the redeeming encouragement of the Holy Spirit, and angels as common and ordinary as my teammate Jim, who wrap arms around us, and say, I understand. It is going to be all right.

We are forgiven.

Innocence lost can be hope regained.

# Who's in Your Window?

## Isaiah 6:1-6 and Hebrews 11

> *In this All Saints sermon, I pluck the saints of the Church from the Cloud of Witnesses and relocate them in the sanctuary's stained glass.*

Today is All Saints Day. It is a curious liturgical occasion in our tradition, a bit awkward, even.

Calvin and the Reformers remind us that God alone is to be worshipped, certainly not other human beings, and they did largely away with the medieval understanding of saints as the objects of idolatrous worship. Visit sanctuaries stormed by Reformation mobs and you will soon grow bored with the empty alcoves, the lonely homes of saintly statues ripped away long ago. The Reformers rightly remind us that God is God and we are not. We run great risks deifying other people, alive or dead.

Still, who among us does not know one we would call a saint? Who can look back at the way grace has followed us, and recall the people through whom God has reached out to us, and not think of a few sterling examples of the Christian faith lived? Who can look back at her Christian journey, at the trials and joys of fleeting faith, and not think of a few key people whose example was crucial; when we failed and needed to know that someone would forgive us; when we staggered, and needed direction; when we felt so unloved, and needed unconditional love; when questions crept in and answers crept out, and suddenly nothing in the world made sense, and I feel so lonely and who can believe in God anyway? Where is God now?

The recipients of the letter to the Hebrews might have felt something like this. Their faith was flagging. Their religious practice seemed suddenly empty, hollow.

We are not sure who wrote Hebrews. We do know that he was someone intimately familiar with the Hebrew scriptures. The writer was a person who drew his faith in tough times from the cloud of witnesses, people who had gone before. In times of trial and doubt he recalled the saints of old: Noah, Abraham, Sarah, Isaac, Jacob, Moses, David, Samuel. These were people who had, somehow, someway, weathered their own storms and nonetheless remained faithful to their God. This writer reminded his readers of an amazing possibility: recalling the example of others can be restorative, healing, helpful.

After all, it was not by miracle or by superhuman status or by magic that these paragons of fidelity had made their impact. It was by faith. Trust. Reliance upon God. Devotion to the divine.

If this is the criteria, can we be saints? Are we called, like Isaac, to be more than we think we can be?

Frederick Buechner recalled in a recent interview that he had made a series of speeches in Chattanooga. Someone sent him a local newspaper report soon afterwards. It contained an article describing those speeches, and in it was the line, "Some say we had a saint among us." [17] Buechner was flabbergasted. How, he wondered, could someone call him a saint? He had done nothing except share as honestly as he could a part of himself through his words, disclosed his struggles, his limits, his challenges. A saint?

But, no matter how uncomfortable he was with the title, he later admitted that maybe he is in a way a saint. Like Isaac who said, "Here I am," he realized that all he offered was a gift from God. In fact, his gifts from God were all that he had to offer.

Thus Buechner describes a saint as "one whom, no matter how limited, the power of God shows through." Surely John Calvin would not mind, for we see saints not as gods, but as real, every day, common people who exude their faith so honestly that it cannot help but shine on others.

I look back on the power of God shown through to me, from my childhood, through so many, so many, well, saints. I remember those who took it seriously when they promised at a child's baptism to raise the child in the ways of Christ. I remember Christian brothers and sisters who took it seriously when we affirmed our essential unity at the Lord's Table. I remember not the perfect, the guiltless, the haloed, the self-righteous. I remember rather the honest, the persistent, the gracious, the kind. I remember people who wrestled with grace on my account.

---

[17] Stephen Kendrick, "On Spiritual Autobiography: An Interview with Frederick Buechner," *The Christian Century,* Vol. 109,14o. 29 (Oct. 1992), 900-903.

There was nothing magic about them. There was, instead, a quiet dignity and a sense that their faith could someday be mine, if I had the fortitude to walk their footsteps.

My family moved across the state from my home congregation when I was a high school senior. I could not have foreseen the difficulty in leaving my childhood saints.

In our new congregation there was a woman of some means. Joye Thomas and her husband had been key leaders in the congregation. Their commitment and faith had helped keep that congregation alive. Joye decided that she wanted to give the church a set of beautiful stained-glass windows. The session agreed to receive the windows. They found the artist. They picked out several Bible stories and symbols to be depicted.

The largest window, and the grandest, was to be in the entrance hall to the sanctuary. It was to span the entire vestibule. It would be the first sight as one entered to worship and the final thought as one emerged back into the world. It was decided that this huge and gorgeous window would depict the Parable of the Good Samaritan. The church waited excitedly to see the finished window. It was soon complete. An exquisite work of art – Tiffany style – it depicted surely enough the Parable of the Good Samaritan.

But something was different. Wrong, even. You could easily identify each of the story's characters, only there was an extra character, someone depicted in the window who is not in the Biblical story. A woman. Standing to the side, in a prominent position in the window, she smiles gracefully at the beaten and robbed traveler.

That woman was Joye Thomas's mother.

My first reaction was horror. What audacity, I thought, what arrogance to rewrite a Biblical parable merely to get her mother's face up in lights! Joye had changed the story.

Or had she?

Perhaps the story had changed her.

By placing her mother in that story, Joye was paying tribute to the saints. It was her way of saying that had it not been for her mother, she would never had understood the Parable of the Good Samaritan, or maybe even the Parable of the Prodigal Son, or maybe even Jesus himself. Perhaps her mother in that window, lodged between the Samaritan and tiffany roses, was a testament of faith that would have been impossible without the example of Joye's mother.

I came to see that window in a different light. That window offered a Technicolor vision of what is possible with faith; that all of us are called to be saints, people 'whom, no matter how little, the power of God shows through.'

That is what the writer of Hebrews is up to. He invites us to imagine our own windows, that we might draw faith from the examples of those we would place in it. He invites us to scan our lives for those moments, those people, those saints who taught us by example the unconditional love of Jesus Christ; who showed us, what Jesus would have us do; who envisioned us not as we were then, but as what we were capable of being through Jesus Christ.

Who in your life would you label a saint?

Who fills your cloud of witnesses?

Who would you place in your stained-glass window, the power of God shining through?

# Choosing Jesus in a Starbucks World

## Matthew 4:1-11

*This sermon was preached at a national stewardship conference. The temptation of Jesus seems an odd text for such an occasion, yet ...*

Being a parent has given me some small perspective on the God's view of God's children. That is because children, like grownups, have minds of their own. With minds of our own, we like to do what we want to do, not necessarily what others want us to do.

Which is why I am usually a grim failure when I order one of my kids to do something. "Because I said so" only raises their hackles and my blood pressure. So, since ordering a kid to do something rarely works, I often resort to persuasion. It is far better to be persuasive than directive. And if persuasion does not work, well, try being sneaky. Stealthy. Underhanded.

Try offering choices. When I want my six-year-old son to do something, I give him carefully crafted choices. I honor his autonomy – he still gets to choose – but I funnel his behavior by narrowing his options. Let me illustrate.

Kids really must bathe. Bathing is good. Nonetheless, my son thinks bathing is a waste of time. I have stopped growling that "it is time for a bath, and like it or not, in five minutes, you had better be in the tub. Or else." This approach does not work.

Here is another approach. "Wow," I say. "You are such a big boy, you get to choose. You can decide for yourself to take a bath, or a shower. Which do you choose?" This method really works. Sometimes.

But other times, Ian looks at me and says, "Television." "Corn dog" makes the occasional appearance.

I give him option A and B, and he chooses C. I offer C or D, and he opts for F. That is how it goes with kids.

That is how it goes with humanity. God sets us amidst clear choices, focuses our attention on decisions which are life-affirming, on choices which are community-sustaining, and sometimes, still, we set ourselves right outside the box.

Religious people have long pondered this human impulse to multiply our options. Explaining this impulse lay at the center of the creation story. Or creation *stories*. There are two creation stories, of course.

In the first, in Genesis' first chapter, God orders the chaos. In neat, sequential steps, God brings what was disparate and tangled and places them in lovely order. Then, on the seventh day, pleased with the garden and all that surrounds it, God rests.

In the second story, the one in Genesis' second and third chapters, humanity has a bit more personality. God has created the world such that human beings may live safely, and joyfully, with one another and with God. That human beings are to live within boundaries is clear; God places a tree in the garden. My son Ian might call that tree option C. It is on the other side of the parentally filtered options. What God has ordered and given in joy, humanity wants somehow to reach beyond. By reaching beyond the choices, Adam and Eve tilt the cosmos back towards chaos.

That is how it goes with humanity. God sets us amidst clear choices, focuses our attention on decisions which are life-affirming, on choices which are community-sustaining, and sometimes, still, we set ourselves right outside of the garden.

Or at least we are tempted to. Temptation is the allure of choices outside God's intentions for us.

Jesus was tempted. Like those before him, Jesus retreats from the city and its choices and withdraws to the simplicity of the desert. Like Noah's family, floating forty days atop the waters, rising above the complexity; like Moses and the Israelites, meandering forty years in the desert, remembering again that only God provides reliable options; Jesus confronts his temptations when he removes himself to simplicity.

Someone said once that he was not certain who discovered water, but he was pretty sure it was not a fish. The most obvious temptations are often too subtle to be noticed because we are surrounded by them. We see them only from a distance. So Jesus retreats to confront his temptations. They are three.

To turns stones to bread and feed to hungry people.

To throw himself from the temple, creating a public display of God's protection, just the credential he needs to bring attention to his message.

To rule the world. Imagine the good to be done with such power.

We think of temptation as the devil sitting on our shoulder, beguiling us to evil, pulling us towards immorality. This is not what happens with Jesus. Jesus is not tempted to evil. Jesus is tempted to compromise. Each temptation he confronts is a worthy thing. Which is precisely why such options are tempting. Feeding hungry people, teaching attentive crowds, wielding political power for good – most would jump at the chance. Any of them. All of them. But none of these roles completes the incarnational promise.

Jesus' temptation is to be good enough, to meet people's expectations (but not God's).

So Jesus does a striking thing. Jesus limits his options. He reduces his choices. The incarnate Christ minimizes his alternatives. If he is to be completely faithful, there are options no longer open to him. Feeding the world, ruling the world, dazzling the world, they are no longer options. For Jesus has come to redeem the world.

This temptation story is common to Mark and Luke's gospels, as well as Matthew's. It is that important. The Bible is teaching us something about the characteristics of temptation. It is the nature of the human heart to broaden its autonomy. We long to enhance and to extend our freedom. Our instinct is to increase and widen our options.

Yet it may be, paradoxically, that unbridled choice actually limits us. Unbounded options may be, in fact, spiritually debilitating.

Barry Schwartz has written an insightful little book. It is called *The Paradox of Choice: Why More is Less*. The book's central thesis is that our consumerist society has produced so many products between which we may choose that we are becoming paralyzed by complexity. Faced with so many choices in the marketplace, we are intellectually frozen.

Because it is in our nature to broaden our autonomy, to extend our freedom, to maximize our choices, you would think that more choice will make us happy. It does not. Survey after survey demonstrates that Americans are not as happy as we were forty years ago. Schwartz argues that the complex matrix of day-to-day choices has conspired to reduce our happiness, to make us uneasy. He argues that such extensive choice makes us question our decisions, even before we make them. It gives us unrealistically high expectations. It can come even to make us blame ourselves for our failures.

And, paradoxically, too much choice leads us to feel out of control.

Which is counter intuitive, is not it? We assume that greater choice leads to greater sense of control. After all, if one has only two choices, it is hard to think that she has much control. If she had fifteen choices, why, then she would have a greater sense of control. With so many options, exercising her autonomy would lend itself to a sense of mastery and power.

But it does not work that way. Schwartz summarizes an overwhelming consensus of social science research that shows that the greater the options, the less the sense of control. Yet we continue, producing more products, offering more options, pursuing ever greater variety.

I have a friend who visited Blockbuster Videos to select a movie for the evening. He had no particular movie in mind when he entered. He would browse, then choose. Thirty minutes later he left. Empty handed. The variety of choices paralyzed him.

Have you visited a grocery store and surveyed the variety of breakfast cereals? Tooth paste? Do you remember the simple days when Baskin Robbins ice cream bragged about its 31 flavors? 31 flavors? How quaint!

Have you visited Starbucks Coffee? Here is what Starbuck's homepage brags:

"When you consider our milk options, number of shots, various syrups and the choice of whip or no-whip, we have up to 87,000 different drink combinations – all customized to your own individual needs." [18]

All customized. Individual needs.

Should not that bring happiness?

My niece recently graduated from college. She does not know what she wants to do. She is preparing to take the LSAT and the MCAT. She does not know if she wants to be a doctor, or a lawyer, or either, so she will take the tests. Whichever test brings the higher score, she will pursue.

Her car sports a bumper sticker. It says, "I took the road less traveled. Now, where in hell am I?"

All customized. Individual needs. Should not that bring happiness?

Is someone in your family wading through the dizzying array of Medicare pharmaceutical options? Is it bringing them happiness?

---

[18] http://www.starbucks.com/retail/nutrition_info.asp.

And let us not think that the religious world is immune from this ubiquity of choice.

A college friend bragged that she was christened Catholic as an infant, baptized Baptist as a teen, and in college was studying Judaism. She wanted to be prepared to go to any direction when she met her husband.

In this post-denominational world, many people choose churches like they choose cars. We find a church that meets our needs. All customized. Individualized. Then, if we must, we can trade it in for another church.

And churches which seem best at marketing religion as product – and then growing! – are also the churches likeliest to present a religion of reduced choices. They simplify the gospel. They reduce faith to a bare and narrow spectrum. As Schwartz puts it, "conservative denominations … are attractive in part because they limit the choices people face in other parts of their lives." [19]

I do not want to emulate these churches. Yet, I wonder if their numeric success is partially explained by their giving people tools which reduce the number of options in a complex world.

If temptation is the allure of choices outside God's intentions for us, is it possible that one of modern life's chief temptations is the impulse to create more choice than it is good for us to have? Is it possible that our choice to create choices actually distracts us from God?

---

[19] Barry Schwartz, *The Paradox of Choice: Why More is Less*, New York: Harper Collins, 2004, p. 40.

# Jesus, Jekyll, and Hyde

## Matthew 23:1-15

*Peter Marshall introduced a Scottish-style worship service to the American church in the 1940s. It is called the Kirkin' o' the Tartan. I have preached many of these services, which can tend to such national celebration so as to be trite. The goal, then, is to remain Biblical while also honoring the church's history in the Scottish context.*

Did that scripture reading sound a bit severe? "But woe to you, scribes and Pharisees, hypocrites!"

Our Scottish forbearers were accustomed to sermons on scripture readings like this one. One day a Scottish preacher went on and on about hell. "It will be awful," he said. "It will be painful," he continues. "There will be much gnashing of teeth," he promised.

An old man on the front pew looked up and smiled broadly, smacking his gums. He had no teeth.

The preacher looked him square and replied, "Teeth will be provided."

Welcome to Kirkin' – a celebration of all thing Scottish masquerading as a worship service. Despite my skepticism, it is nonetheless worth thinking about, how Scottish Presbyterianism has shaped our contemporary religious sensibilities. And this morning I have an idea. I think it is possible to illustrate a central religious impulse of the Scottish soul by taking an imaginary walking tour of downtown Edinburgh.

That impulse? An impatience with hypocrisy.

And where to start our tour? The High Street, just as it meets Waverly Train Station, Edinburgh's main transportation hub.

When I moved to Edinburgh in 1989, it was from Waverly that I emerged to begin my student life. Just outside Waverly a Scottish vendor always parked his cart, selling Scottish trinkets and specialties. A poignant sign was hung above his merchandise. It read, "English Spoken. American Understood."

The Scots are a proud people, lacking neither confidence nor a sense of identity. They are subtle – mostly – plainspoken, direct. They are neither florid nor fancy. Rather, they are understated, unassuming.

We dress in reds and blues. They dress in grays and browns.

In Scotland, this joke is a big hit. Why do Americans talk so loudly? So they can be heard over their clothing.

Yes, the Scots prefer understated directness. Simplicity. Frankness.

And they are impatient with hypocrisy. They like their literature this way, too. Just blocks away from Waverly Train Station was born one of Scotland's literary giants, Robert Louis Stevenson. You remember *Treasure Island*. All told, Stevenson wrote twelve novels and novellas. Stevenson's father was a minister in the Church of Scotland. "Now I often wonder," Stevenson said late in his life, "what I inherited from this old minister. I must suppose, indeed, that he was fond of preaching sermons, and so am I, though I never heard it maintained that either of us loved to hear them."

From Stevenson's birthplace it is only a brisk walk to St. Giles Church. St. Giles is the High Kirk, or the High Church, of Scotland. Its central four pillars have stood for 900 years. John Knox preached at St Giles. Knox brought Protestantism to Scotland in the 1550s. If he had not done what he did, we might not be worshipping here today, as we are, where we are, in the way that we are.

When Knox died in 1572 they buried him in the church graveyard. In a symbol of something or other, the graveyard is now a parking lot. John Knox, the father of Scottish Presbyterianism, is buried under space 23.

But above the asphalt, looking down upon space 23 and therefore down upon Knox's grave, is a statue of James VI. James VI of Scotland, that is. In England they remember him as James I. He was the first king of the United Kingdom. Scotland had been independent before that, free from England. James VI was therefore seen as a traitor.

Which is why that statue of James VI has a strange feature. On the nape of James' neck, maybe four inches tall, barely visible unless you know to look for it, is a small face. While the statue looks east, this face looks west. And whose face is this? Like the front of the statue, it is also the face of King James. The small addition was the sculptor's way of saying that James VI was two-faced.

The Scots are impatient with hypocrisy.

From St. Giles, if you will walk just west to the next corner, where the Royal Mile intersects The Mound, you will see a famous pub – Deacon Brodie's. The pub has become an Edinburgh landmark. Deacon Brodie's pub is named for a real historical figure. Deacon Brodie, whose given name was William Brodie, was an 18th century Edinburgh resident. He was wealthy, famous, and powerful, deacon of the Incorporation of Wrights and Masons. He socialized with Edinburgh's rich and powerful, meeting with poet Robert Burns and painter Sir Henry Raeburn. He was well known, and broadly respected, until the city found out.

At night, you see, Brodie had another life, a secret life, an altogether different life. By night, Brodie was a burglar, and a gambler, and myth came to have it, a body snatcher. He used his professional position to gain access to the wealthy, and he made wax impressions of their housekeys. Then, when darkness came, and the time was right, he stole and robbed and plundered. He used his ill-gotten gains to support two mistresses, who did not know the other, and the five children he fathered between them. And he gambled. He gambled a lot.

By day, then, Brodie was upstanding, respected, and privileged. By night he was a thief and a liar. In other words, he said one thing and did another, and by now you have gotten my point, that Scots hate hypocrisy.

Is it any surprise then that Robert Louis Stevenson created a character based on Deacon Brodie? Deacon Brodie was the real-life inspiration for Stevenson's Jekyll and Hyde. The *Strange Case of Dr Jekyll and Mr Hyde* was Stevenson's bestselling novella about a man with a split personality. Good and bad, right and wrong, respected and reviled – all at the same time.

*Dr Jekyll and Mr Hyde* has been seen as a commentary on the duality of human nature. It has been seen as a treatise on psychology, pre-Freud. Some have seen *Jekyll and Hyde* as a harsh commentary on Victorian repression. I see *Jekyll and Hyde* as yet another installment in the Scottish impatience with hypocrisy. You see, in their understated, plainspoken way, the Scots picture a better way of living, one of simple honesty, dignified integrity, and of religious consistency.

Have you heard about the Scottish atheist fishing on Loch Ness? Nessie suddenly attacked his boat and tipped it over. Nessie was about to eat him when the man shouted, "Save me, God!" Suddenly time was frozen, and the man hung inches from Nessie's dripping teeth. A voice from heaven came; "I thought you did not believe in me."

The man replied, "Aw God, Gie's (give me) a break! Thirty seconds ago, I did not believe in the Loch Ness Monster, either!"

The Scottish instinct for plainspoken consistency is expressed in its religious life. Scottish Presbyterianism finds its impatience with religious hypocrisy in holy scripture.

Go home this afternoon. Pull out your concordance or find an online concordance. Look for the words "hypocrite" or "hypocrisy" in the four Gospels. You will be astonished at how frequently they appear. And generally, Jesus is the one using these words. Jesus hated hypocrisy. He loved hypocrites, but he hated hypocrisy. He hoped for – and modeled for us – lives of consistence, authenticity, and integrity. Jesus painted a living picture of synchronized belief *and* action. He offered wisdom that could be trusted *and* lived. And Jesus confronted anyone who was pretending to be one type of person by day but another by night, pretending to be one type of person in public and another in private.

Jesus even confronted the religious authorities of his day. He said that the rabbis bound others up in high expectations, then did nothing to help them. He told people to do as the rabbis *said*, but not as they *did*. Jesus called the rabbis hypocrites. They loved public attention. They loved the prestige of position. They loved the head table and the black-tie affairs and the titles and the robes and you have no idea how uncomfortable it is for me to read this passage.

But lest you feel too smug about Jesus roasting us preacher types, Jesus next says something astonishing. He says that we – all of us – are students. What is more, we have but one instructor: the messiah.

And finally, most poignantly, he says that the lesson we are most to learn is simply said and harder done: "the greatest among you will be your servant. All who exalt themselves will be humbled, and all who humble themselves will be exalted."

Jesus did not stop with an angry critique of hypocrisy. No, he offered a way out and up. He said that hypocrisy's loving antidote is becoming a servant. If hypocrisy is the disease, service is the cure. And that is true for everyone. Because we are all students. All of us are travelers. All of us are trying day in and month out to live gospel values and to serve the least of these, our sisters and brothers in need.

And that is a great tradition which streams to us from Scotland. Scotland built its identity upon the common person. This is a grand *leveling*, this insistence that Christian grand and meek, this religious affection for the common person, that comes to us largely from our Scottish ancestry.

The Old Testament prophets decried a religious elite detached from the needs of common people. Jesus railed against religious officials blind to the troubles of the poor. Scottish Presbyterianism was birthed in the passionate insistence that all citizens – lords and ladies, serfs and masters – all citizens were equally fellow travelers wandering together towards God. Authentic religion, then, could not abide hypocrisy. What we do is related to what we believe, no matter how conscious of it we are. The call, then, the *religious* call, is to match creed and deed, to pair faith with action, to combine word with lifestyle. The call is to live Monday as we do on Sunday, to live by night as we do by day.

Less Hyde. More Jekyll. More Jesus.

Today is one for pageant and finery. Oh, how I love it. The bagpipes. The drums. The haggis. The kilts. When I moved home from Scotland I spoke to a Rotary Club. In the question and answer period afterwards, someone asked if it were true, what they say about what Scotsmen wear under their kilts. "I do not know," I replied. "I never looked."

What a tremendous day, this Kirkin,', this celebration of all things Scottish.

And if we are to be true to the instincts of the Kirk which gave its rise, we must know that this pageantry is not an end to itself. Today's pageantry is meant for something larger, meant to be the beginning of something, not the end. Inspired by our worship of God, we are meant now to be humbled, that as we leave this sanctuary we do so not as puffed up Presbyterians but rather as awed and humbled servants.

Robert Burns is the most beloved of Scottish poets, and Burns was no fan of the Church of Scotland. He saw too much hypocrisy in it. In a critique of religion that I suspect makes Jesus smile, Burns once described authentic religion. It was not one of pomp nor of finery but expressed in a simple Cotter's hut.

We are fellow travelers, you and I, with one instructor, and one father. Imagine the authentic religious life, passionate, pure, and holy.

As Burns says it,

> *Compar'd with this, how poor Religion's pride,*
> *In all the pomp of method, and of art;*
> *When men display to congregations wide*
> *Devotion's ev'ry grace, except the heart!*
> *The Power, incens'd, the pageant will desert,*
> *The pompous strain, the sacerdotal stole;*
> *But haply, in some cottage far apart,*
> *May hear, well-pleas'd, the language of the soul;*
> *And in His Book of Life the inmates poor enroll.* [20]

---

[20] Robert Burns, *The Cotter's Saturday Night*, 1786.

# Saints and Sweethearts

## Song of Solomon 4:8-11, 8:6-7 and I John 4:7-12

*This sermon, preached on a Sunday preceding Valentine's Day,
contextualized the longing for love within the larger longing for
God. I am indebted to Frank Yates for this sermon's inspiration
and much of its exegesis.*

There is much to be said for the single life. Jesus remained
single! Most of Jesus' disciples were single. Singleness can be a sacred
and faithful lifestyle for Christians. We sometimes forget that in our
praise for family values.

Still, there is within many of us a deep longing, a fiery yearning
for companionship. And not just for common companionship, but
for love. And not just love in a general, the next-person-who-comes-
through-the-door sense. For many people, there is a passionate
desire to share love with a specific person, regardless of whether we
have yet met him or her. For some, fairy tale princes and princesses
describe this reality. The radio croons about it. Soap operas depict
it. Bookstores have entire sections dedicated to romantic novels it.
Match.com and Yahoo Personals and eHarmony arrange it. This
impulse is for many one of life's deepest and most basic desires.

Would you be surprised to learn that the Church recognizes this
longing for love? There is in our history the legend of a saint who
was executed by a Roman emperor in the third century. As a young
priest this someday-saint served under the evil Emperor Claudius II.
The Emperor needed men for his many wars, but people grew tired
of continually sending their young men off to fight. Wives and
fiancées began to resist involuntary conscription and encouraged
their lovers to hide. They dodged the draft! An angry Claudius
declared a temporary ban on marriages and even engagements. But
this priest, this Father Valentine, continued quietly, secretly, to
perform marriages. For his disobedience he was imprisoned and
executed.

Was this the Valentine whose name is lent to this week's
celebration of love? Church records are unclear. There are as many
as eight martyrs with the name Valentine. Another legend claims that
a Valentine, held in prison, fell in love with the jailer's daughter and
sent her letters signed "From your Valentine."

Will the real Valentine please stand up?

We cannot know exactly which Valentine the early church plucked from its records for February 14. What we do know is how and why the Church created Valentine's Day. I bet you thought Valentine's Day was created by florists and greeting card companies. No. It was the Church.

You see, the early Church faced a scandal. Christianity was suddenly the religion of the Roman Empire. The Romans continued celebrating a pagan festival called Lupercalia, and it was raucous. Each year, on February 14, the people of Rome took to the streets with wine wearing only their loin cloths. Their festival was designed to insure their sheep's fertility and to cure any barrenness in the city. The young men, scantily clad, ran about the city tapping the women of Rome. (By the way, the entire ritual was supposedly intended to keep the wolves out of the city - wink wink.) To the Church it looked very much like an excuse for something altogether different, which was quite an embarrassment.

For an answer to this scandal the Church went to the books. No, I do not mean the Bible. I mean that the Church went to its history records. There were found the records of eight martyrs named Valentine. Who could replace Lupercalia? The most compelling Christian equivalent was perhaps the legend of the marrying priest executed by the evil Claudius? Thus, began Valentine's Day.

But there is more. During Lupercalia, the Romans placed the names of young women in a box. (Gloria Steinhem would rightfully have a fit!) Young men drew the names and would, for the next year, be matched as protectors and companions for the names of those drawn. The Church had to do something about this wanton display of matchmaking and debauchery. The answer was simple! Replace the names of young women with the names of the saints of the Church! Then, men would copy, for the next year, the life and qualities of the saint they had drawn.

Uhm ... well ... I have a question for you. Pretend you are 18. You have a choice. On one hand you may choose saintliness. On the other, you might opt for a sweetheart. Which are you going to choose? It did not take long. We do not know just when people rebelled against the saints-in-a-box idea. We do know that by the Middle Ages people were back to sweethearts on Valentine's Day.

Why does religion so often force people to choose between saintliness and sweethearts? What is it about this deep, natural longing for romantic companionship that for so many generates feelings of guilt that seem incompatible with faithfulness? Must we choose? Reformed Christians have always said no. John Calvin, our earliest Reformer, was himself married. We have proclaimed from the start that marriage and love can be key components in our faithfulness to God.

Friday is Valentine's Day. It has become for some a trite occasion. I have an idea. *Let us reChristianize Valentine's Day. Let us use Valentine's Day to connect two of our most basic impulses: our longing for love, and our craving to know God?* Should not Valentine's Day be a chance to remember that God knows us so well that God has given us a holy relationship within which to express and quench our longing for love? Why not *celebrate* that Christians do not have to choose between saintliness and a sweetheart? Let us use Valentine's Day as a chance for our church to celebrate marriages, especially marriages of long standing, to honor and affirm them. Let us *celebrate* our longing for love!

Which leads me to the Song of Solomon. The Song of Solomon is a love poem. The same people who brought us saints-in-a-box tried to tell us that this book is really about God's love for Israel or Christ's love for the Church. It is neither. It is a love poem written between a young man and a young woman. Since "absence makes the heart grow fonder," he pleads with her to come down from the high peaks of those Lebanon mountains. "Come with me from Lebanon, my bride," he begs. She is inaccessible to him, but her distance seems only to deepen his longing for her. "You have ravished my heart, my sister, my bride." Young love can overwhelm, take one's heart away. So the young lover cries out, "Your love is better than wine!"

But it is not just the man who feels this painful separation, this longing for love. His lover does, too. In another part of the poem she even risks her life as she wanders around the streets at night looking for her man. She, too, pleads for her lover to come away with her to the vineyard where they can feel the warmth of the other's embrace. She, too, is ravished by love and she laments, "I am sick with love." Their longing is intense, almost violent.

Can this be healthy? Is this allowed? Some rabbis long ago said that the Song of Solomon was too powerful for the immature to even read or touch. Scholars have rated it "PG," and some even "R." Some have even said that it is too "dirty" to be in the Bible! Yet I think God - even though God is never mentioned in the book - speaks an important word to us in the Song of Solomon. God speaks a word to us about gracious gifts. We learn that our longing for our romantic partners can be a holy and beautiful thing. We learn in the Song of Solomon that God understands our longing and in fact blesses it.

We long for love. It is nothing to be ashamed of, afraid of. It is not to be repressed. It is, in fact, to be celebrated! It is part of who we are.

And who are we? What are human beings *for*? The first question in the Westminster Shorter Catechism is, "What is man's chief end?" The answer, of course, is that human beings "are to *love* God and to enjoy God forever." Even more basic than our longing for romantic love is our craving to know and to love and to enjoy Almighty God. So what? you wonder. "Beloved, let us love one another, because love is from God; everyone who loves is born of God and knows God. ... for God is love." That is how 1 John says it. We are to love one another because God, who is love, has loved us.

What might we say, then, about Valentine's Day? What would a modern fusion of sweethearts and saintliness look like?

I have been desperately anxious about this sermon. My anxiety is not about discussing romantic love and sex in the pulpit. We have discussed subjects much touchier than these. Instead, my anxiety has been how to affirm marriage and romantic love when not everyone is married, or in love, or even wants to be. How are we to celebrate Valentine's Day in a way that does not exclude those who are divorced, or single, or widowed? Will this discussion leave a sense that I do not belong in the Church if I have no love or lover to celebrate? I pray that it will not.

Instead, I suggest that Valentine's Day not be only a celebration of love and lovers. I suggest that a Christian approach would make Valentine's Day a celebration also of *longing* for love. Perhaps this day is a time to remember the pastoral word that, for those who are single, divorced, or widowed, God understands your longings. And even if those longings are not to be fulfilled soon, if at all, they are longings which God endorses and understands.

And for those who are in love, our romantic relationships do more than quench our thirst for one another. Our first call in life is always to love and serve God. Marriage, then, is a means to that end. Many think that marriage is God's gift in order that we have children and families. And that is true. Sometimes. Others think that marriage is to keep us from loneliness. And that is true, sometimes. Still others see marriage in psychological terms. It is a way for us jointly to achieve self-realization. Our spouses are our personal companions on the road to completeness. And that can be true. Sometimes.

Yet God gives us marriage for an even greater reason than these. God gives us marriage as a tool for faithfulness. Our longing for love is most holy when it directs us beyond itself to God. For those who are married, marriage is in fact a servant of faithfulness. What is romantic love for? Why did God give us this longing for love? Because, when directed and quenched, this longing for love is yet one more ingredient, one additional tool, to help us in faithfulness.

It is this vision of love we celebrate on Valentine's. It is Jimmy and Rosalyn Carter reading the Bible together each night before they go to sleep. In Spanish. It is Bill and Birdie Lytle, after retirement from years as pastor and spouse, a time you would think would be for relaxation, giving their time as Volunteers in Mission. It is couples in this church who begin each day with a time of quiet devotional reading and prayer. It is her willingness to watch the kids, so he can participate in a community service organization. It is his willingness to pick up everything and move so she can follow God's call to ministry.

It is a vision for love which points beyond itself to God, and it is holy.

So let us celebrate love, and our longing for love, for God is love.

# When to Look Up, or, Learning Which Asses to Listen To

## Numbers 22: 22-38

*This baccalaureate address was preached to the graduating class of Austin College, a Presbyterian-related liberal arts college in Texas, at its Baccalaureate Service.*

President Page, Chairman Johnson, members of the Board of Trustees, Dean Imhoff, distinguished faculty, honored guests, and most poignantly, members of Austin College's Class of 2009, but also your parents, and your kid brothers and sisters, uncles and aunts, and everyone else whose patience and sacrifice have nurtured you to this moment – thank you. I am honored to be here tonight – honored, surprised, and maybe just a little embarrassed.

You see, I did not attend Austin College. I attended Trinity, your sister Presbyterian school in San Antonio. My twin sister Kristi was the first in our family to attend Austin College. Two nieces followed. With such Kangaroo connections my family will tease me as forever as an Austin College wannabe, a pretender.

Baccalaureate services originated in the late Middle Ages. Austin College continues this tradition presumably as an expression of your conviction that faith without ideas is dead, and even more subversively, your conviction that ideas without faith can be deadly. Faith and reason are good partners because knowledge and wisdom are not the same things. Knowledge must be linked to virtue, and God connects the two. Your being here indicates that apparently there are those who still believe this.

This month just happens to mark the exact point in my life when there are as many years this side of college graduation as the other. It is an interesting perch from which to reconnoiter. What I will say tonight is in many ways personal, introspective, and perhaps even a bit autobiographical. I intend, then, a conversation with the graduating class. The rest of you are invited to listen in.

I remember the day my parents delivered me to Trinity. We lugged my spartan belongings upstairs to my dorm room. Then we went out for the last supper. On the way back to the dorm I braced for the final farewell, the shedding of tears, for my mother's outburst at the departure of her youngest son. I got out of the car, ready for the worst. I shut the car door. And Dad … drove away. My parents never even got out of the car. I had previewed that moment as *my* liberation. Apparently, they had, too.

I remember being eighteen. Life bursts with choices at eighteen. Options seem limitless. We scan the horizon left to right and there are so few obstructions. The future is broad, wide, and unfocused. So many universities between which to choose. So many classes from which to decide. So many majors one might declare, so many friends from which to pluck just the right ones. So many professions on the table, so many potential partners to get to know.

Now you are graduating. You have crossed a threshold without perhaps knowing it. Your choice of Austin College may well have been the first in a coming series of choices designed by life to focus you, to direct you, to funnel your energy and passion in one direction and not another.

Think about it. You chose Austin College and not the University of Texas and not Rhodes and not Trinity. You chose one major and not another. You decided upon one career cluster and not others. The time will come when you might choose one life partner and leave behind other options, decide upon one city and sink roots there, choose one style of being in the world and step away from the funky eclectic student lifestyle. Your choices now will focus you, direct you, sharpen you. They will center your gaze on a much narrower horizon point than you might have imagined four years ago.

Is it possible to make these coming choices in such a way that the boundaries they naturally establish empower you, not ensnare you, funnel you, not fence you, liberate you and not trap you?

I am guessing that at some point someone on this campus said to you that education makes us more useful to God. That is a win-win proposition. God knows what you have been made for. Your job is to figure it out and do it. Education helps. The challenge is to know ourselves as well as God does, which is of course impossible, so maybe the more realistic goal is learning to listen for God's dreams for us.

This can be very difficult because so often, we prefer our dreams to God's.

I have chosen as our text the story of Balaam and his talking donkey. That is right; Eddie Murphy is not history's first donkey with attitude and Shrek is not the first protagonist saddled with a comic sidekick. People who say the Bible is boring have not read it.)

On the surface Balaam's story is quite straightforward. He is not unlike Jonah whom God commands to go one direction only Jonah sails another. In that story, God uses a giant fish to redirect the prophet. In this story, a talking donkey does the trick.

The trick is this: a foreign prophet is selling out for cash and prestige and is on his way presumably to curse God's people. God must turn Balaam from his intentions to curse the Israelites and choose instead to bless them. But Balaam is determined, so focused on his own path that he does not see God's sword-swinging angel planted just in front of him. But his donkey does. Twice. Two times the donkey protects Balaam. But, Balaam whips him for his trouble.

The third time is different. The walls close in. Balaam can turn neither left nor right. He is trapped. His path has led him to a dead-end. Balaam's donkey speaks. The irony is comic; a donkey can see more clearly than the professional seer. Because the donkey sees, and speaks, Balaam finally looks up, and sees the angel, and hears the Lord, and finally, finally, finally Balaam gets it. Balaam can now say only what God wants him to say. Seeing how he can be useful to God, nothing else compares. Balaam, a foreign prophet serving a Moabite king, will bless the people God has blessed.

This passage has at least two messages for us tonight.

The first rests in its graphic depiction of a person trapped by two walls and unable to turn left or right. Balaam knows what God asked him to do but Balaam walked a different path. Why? His superiors told him to. And they offered him honor. And they promised him money. Selling out has a long history. Contrary to popular myth, selling out is actually the world's oldest profession. Balaam knows God's dreams for him and he chases his own dreams anyway.

No one can know God's dreams for you, no one but you. Oh, some will think they know, and there will be plenty willing to use you for their own dreams. Still, in the end, only you can amplify God's still small voice whispering the Divine's grand vision for your life. And, unless you are extraordinarily unique, God's path for you will not always be clear and well lit. You will misstep, detour. You might wander the paths of your boss or maybe the paths of your parents or perhaps your own paths which you confuse for God's – ambition or greed or co-dependence.

Nonetheless, God, this gracious God of ours will stay after you, this persistent God will haunt you and help you, will nudge you and nourish you, will come to you in whispers, and if necessary, will send an angel or three, and even after all this, if your ear is still deaf and your eyes remain closed tight and you find yourself dead-still, trapped between walls of your own construction, stuck in a spiritual cul de sac, even then God will do anything to get you to look up.

You will be stunned by the asses through whom God can speak.

I have a friend just a bit older than I am. He made top grades in the engineering department at the University of Michigan, no small feat. From there he joined the good people at Ford Motor Company who quickly saw what they had. Ford fast-tracked my friend. They paid for his MBA. It was not long before my friend was climbing the corporate ladder. It was by most accounts a breathtaking ascent. A six-figure salary. An office at World Headquarters. Keys to the executive washroom.

Then, a tap on the shoulder. The voice said, "Please put any personal belongings in this box and come with me."

What an ass!

My friend had driven to work that morning in a Ford owned vehicle, so there he sat, his box on his lap, waiting for a ride home, dead still. It was one of many coming moments when he would look up.

He told me he had always sensed a call to ministry, as far back as high school. But he was good at math, and his father worked at Ford, and his grandfather had too. The money was good.

Sometimes the wrong paths are tree-lined and manicured.

My friend graduated seminary last year.

I have another friend, in his 60s now. He loves kids. Always has. After college he became a school teacher. It was not long before the family business hit a rough patch and he went home to help. His family owned a beer distributorship, and I will hand it to you that to some young men, distributing beer sounds like the dream job. My friend's dream job was working with kids, though. Nonetheless, my friend took seriously his task and he did it well. A year became two became a decade, then more. He turned that business around, way around.

In his mid-50s he sold his portion of that business to other family members. Then he reignited the flames of God's dreams for him. He and his wife established a foundation supporting work to improve the lives of – you guessed it – children. In addition to their foundation they aim to give away half of their income every year.

I have more of these stories, and so do you, which only proves the point: God lifts us over the walls we accidentally build. Remember that if your choices someday seem to trap you.

Balaam's story has another meaning for us tonight. It has to do with God's impulse to bless and with humanity's temptation to curse, to curse even and especially in God's name.

More and more people are coming to think of religion as curse. They look at feuding religious people, at overtly religious strife, at the Middle East and at Ireland and at the festering wounds in the former Yugoslav republics and they listen to talk radio and they attribute a good many of the world's problems to religion. They have a point, at least so far as they see the unbecoming behavior of some religious people. Where they are wrong, of course, is assuming that religious extremists are authentically religious.

Balaam's story is a simple yet elegant reminder that God's impulse is always, always, always for blessing.

God blesses us. God sends angels and sometimes asses to return us to the path of blessing. I have been speaking of the choices you face and about the wisest strategies for making those choices in such a way that they do not come to hem you in.

The wisest strategy, of course, is to ask God's advice first, to listen for God's dreams for you, because in the wide, wide circle of God's love God intends for you never to be trapped but for you always to be blessed.

And blessed for a purpose – that you might bless others.

I find it singularly instructive that as the Israelites make final preparation to inherit the land God has long promised, God does not choose a prophet of their own tribe for their next blessing. It is likewise interesting for those of you now leaving this fine institution. You now erupt from this place to enter a culture increasingly complex and religiously pluralistic. You have certainly heard the oft quoted statistic that there are now more Moslems in the United

States than there are Episcopalians. As you hone your hearts to embrace God's dreams for you, may you do so trusting that God is also at work dreaming within others. Be who you are and allow God the freedom to draw blessings also from others, even if they are different.

We started our time together observing that faith and reason are good partners because knowledge and wisdom are not the same things. I suggested that knowledge must be linked to virtue, and that God connects the two.

God connects knowledge with virtue. This is the point. Blessed by God to be a blessing to the world, you are now prepared to use what you have here learned to make virtuous choices.

May God's blessings inspire your choices.

May you choose to be people of hope, and honor, and *blessing*.

# Bicycling on Custer's Left Flank

John 20.1-18

*This Easter sermon followed a visit to Little Bighorn National Monument, which inspired a conversation about cemeteries.*

Easter has many meanings: forgiveness from sins; the promise of new beginnings, second chances; the promise that God identifies with our pain; our hope for life after death; our anticipated reunion with those who have gone before. Of these many meanings, I want today to thank God for the hope of eternal life with the God who knows our names.

Which has me thinking about death, and about how we remember those who have died, and especially how we remember them by name.

I visited an Ontario cemetery recently, a place I had heard of but had never seen. It is the ancestral burial place for much of my father's family, for generations. After some detective work, I found the cemetery beside a country church. Engraved deep within a weathered and moss-grown stone were words, words my family had long forgotten: the names of my great-great grandfather and great-great grandmother. William Murray. Eliza. I had not known their names. Sometimes, cemeteries remember our names when our descendants do not.

Sometimes not even cemeteries remember our names. A cemetery cannot record what it does not know, after all. Stacy Horn wrote an essay about the indignity of being buried in a Potter's Field. You remember what a Potter's Field is. In Matthew's gospel, Judas is horrified after selling Jesus out. He cannot wait to get rid of his blood money, so he throws it into the temple. The priests use the money, tainted as it is, to buy a field from a potter, and they make the field into a cemetery for, as Horn describes them, "the poor, the unclaimed, the unidentified." People with no money, and often no family or friends, are buried in Potters' Fields.

New York City has had a Potter's Field since 1869; since then, you will never guess how many people have died in that city with neither family nor money. New York's Potter's Field contains the remains of 750,000 people, nameless, faceless, perhaps completely

forgotten, human beings. And the city adds 1,500 to 3,000 every year.
21

Thus far, we have visited two cemeteries, a country graveyard in Ontario and New York City's Potter's Field. You may be thinking, "It's Easter. Why is the preacher going on about death? Is not Easter about life and resurrection and triumph?"

You are right, of course. Easter is about these things. And, yet, if we are to absorb Easter's full joy, we must also understand what we are up against. We cannot understand how tall God is until we understand how far God has knelt to be with us. You see, death is real. Death is our enemy.

Every Sunday many congregations remind themselves of this reality as they conclude the scripture readings. "The grass withers and the flower fades," we opine. Well, we fade too. We wither and we die. Not long ago, on Ash Wednesday, many of you attended worship services which reminded you that we are "dust and to dust we shall return."

This is not happy news. Maybe its unpleasantness explains why our culture averts its eyes from death. Not a century ago we died in our family homes, surrounded by loved ones. Neighbors gathered as the body lay in state in the home. Children would see death, were included in the rituals of death.

Now, we seem averse even to the word death. We prefer euphemisms like "deceased" or "passed away" or "gone home." Many newspapers have stopped printing obituaries in favor of something called "in transition." Death is no longer worthy to headline the obituaries.

I am routinely told by 30-somethings and 40-somethings that, "This is the first funeral I have ever been to." It is as if our entire culture has seen one too many episodes of "The Roadrunner" cartoon. Wylie E. falls off that cliff and slams a coyote-shaped hole in the earth and, still, he picks himself up good as new. Nothing to worry about. Death is not real.

From the make-believe world of violent movies to the institutional way we have come to die, we have not given death its due. We have segmented death, cordoned it off, dealt with it by not dealing with it. And yet, if resurrection is to make sense to us, we

---

21 Stacy Horn, "Potter's Field," National Public Radio/All Things Considered, aired July 25, 2001.

must look at death. Because death is real. The Bible says that death is the enemy. There is nothing intrinsically immortal about us. We will die, and most of us will be forgotten in due time.

Jesus died too. He was really dead. He had slipped into no Rip Van Winkle coma. His heart no longer beat. His lungs filled not with air. His body was prepared for burial by people far more accustomed to seeing death than we are. They knew what they were talking about. Jesus was dead. No pastoral lie could cover the truth. No well-meaning euphemism could salve the wound. He was not in transition. Jesus did not live on "in the hearts of his disciples." He would not be with them forever because of their naive vows "never to forget." Jesus was dead. It was finished. Party over. Last one out, get the lights.

So come with me now to yet another burial place. A tomb stands in the distance. Jesus is laid in it. At least Pilate had allowed the dignity of a proper burial. Joseph of Arimathea took the body and laid it in that tomb, there, just over there.

Wait, who is that? It is Peter, running with another man. We recognize him, but we cannot recall his name. They run to the tomb and peer in. They seem stunned, even confused. The body is not there! The cloth that had been on Jesus' head – it has been rolled up and set aside. Peter and the other disciples believe, but they believe – what? They stumble off, somewhat unsure of what to make of all this.

And Mary – Mary is here too. She sits in the utter exhaustion of loving the Lord with her everything only to have been let down, taken for a ride. It was not true, she thinks. This message of love and grace and of God's consuming passion for the people has gotten itself killed by the world's cruelty and callousness. Just when she thinks she has seen God, he evaporates like a mirage into the midst of her self-delusion. But now she must try to forget, even as she has been forgotten.

Someone approaches her. Who? The gardener? He asks, "Why are you crying? Who are you looking for?" which is after all a reasonable, logical question to ask a weeping woman in a graveyard. Mary, assuming the worst, blurts out at him, "Look, mister, if you have taken the body, the least you can do is tell me where you have put him."

He responds, this man, quietly, gently. He says, "Mary." Jesus recognizes her even from the other side of death. He calls her by name! Mary crumbles in thankful emotion and praise. "Rabbouni," she says, "Rabbouni."

The world may forget, but God in Christ always remembers us, knows us by name.

We talk about death on Easter precisely because we Christians know what is more real, most authentic, and it isn't death. Some wag commented that there are only two sure things in life: death and taxes. Well, he was wrong. Taxes are the only certainty because death has been defeated. Christ is victorious. In Jesus of Nazareth, as Huston Smith points out, God deals with the chief dilemmas of human life: the anxiety of our guilt and the fear of our death!

Frederick Buechner, in his memoir *The Eyes of the Heart,* writes about an imaginary conversation with his long-dead grandmother Naya. And they speak about death. Naya says, "When someone once asked your Uncle Jim if some friend or other had passed away, he answered in his inimitable fashion by saying, 'Passed away? Good God, he is dead.' And I know just how he felt. I always thought passed away was a silly way of putting it..."

Naya continued, "It is the world that passes away," and flutters one hand delicately through the air to show the manner of its passing. [22]

It is the world that is passing away. Not God. Not God's people. God gives us that infinite gift in Christ's death and resurrection.

We have visited three cemeteries so far, in Ontario, New York and in first-century Palestine. Let us drop by just one more. I visited the Little Big Horn, site of Custer's infamous Last Stand. It is a terrible and amazing, heart-breaking, and awe-inspiring place, wonderful and horrible simultaneously. It is like life in that way, full of contradictions, irresolvable tensions.

I took my bicycle with me and rode the distance between the main battlefield and the site where two of Custer's commanders had been pinned down that day, unable to reach the fight. Major Marcus Reno and Captain Frederick Benteen, and their troops, watched and heard the main skirmish from a considerable distance. I peddled that distance, thinking as I rode up and down the small hills that I was

---

[22] Frederick Buechner, *The Eyes of the Heart: a memoir of the lost and found,* New York: Harper Collins.

riding Custer's left flank. Along that road there remain to this day individual crosses, white crosses, marking the exact spots where individual soldiers lost their lives. How, I wondered, do we know the precise locations where individual soldiers died?

On that painful day in 1876, with his arrogance and bravado, Custer led five companies of his own men to their slaughter. Six generations have come and gone since, and those who fought there on both sides are now largely forgotten. Except on the battlefield itself. You see, the battlefield is littered with white headstones marking the very spots of their individual deaths. After the dust cleared that violent day, the Lakota, Cheyenne, and Arapaho collected their dead and burned their warriors' bodies on the scene. That was their custom.

The slain soldiers of the 7th Cavalry, however, lay unprotected to the weather for some days. Reinforcements arrived later to bury the bodies. But the reinforcements were in a rush. They were charged to pursue the military campaign, after all.

You might be amazed by what they did. I was. The hurried soldiers buried their fallen comrades in shallow graves, intending that later the army would send the necessary manpower to unearth their bones and give them a more proper burial. But how in such a hurry could they mark these shallow graves? How could they assure that their dead comrades would be remembered by name, that their bodies would be associated with their names?

The hurried soldiers scribbled the names of the fallen on small pieces of paper and then rolled up those snippets of paper. They stuffed the names into spent shell casings. Then they made crosses from the abandoned teepee lumber of the Lakota, Cheyenne, and Arapaho camp. Finally, at the head of each shallow grave, they dropped the identifying shell casing on the freshly turned soil, and they put the bottom of their makeshift cross atop the casing, and they thrust the shell casings deep into the ground with the points of their makeshift crosses.

The names of the dead were remembered at the foot of the cross. Literally.

Remember the 7th Cavalry.

Now, recall Calvary. Jesus died on Mount Calvary. And our names are written at the bottom of *that* cross. "We have been buried with [Christ] by baptism into death, so that, just as Christ was raised from the dead by the glory of the Father, so we too might walk in newness of life" (Romans 6.4).

Even from the other side of death, Jesus remembers your name, knows your name, knows you.

Mary said it first. We shall say it too. "I have seen the Lord." And that is the Easter message, the Easter hope.

He is Risen!
**He is Risen indeed!**
He is Risen!
**He is Risen indeed!**
He is Risen!
**He is Risen indeed!**

# Three Strikes and You're In

## John 21.1-19

*In a post-resurrection appearance, Jesus invites disciples then and now to embrace our call to feed his sheep.*

You might wonder about the bit at the end of today's Gospel reading. Jesus says to Peter that when Peter is old, he will stretch out his hands and be taken where he does not wish to go. That is a weird tidbit, is it not? Church tradition has it that Peter was crucified, like Jesus. Only Peter told his Roman executioners that he did not deserve to die the same death as Jesus. So Peter asked to be crucified upside down, with his head to the ground. Can you imagine such bravery, such obedience, such discipleship?

Peter. The Rock. The rock upon which Christ built the church.

Church tradition has it that Peter was crucified by the Romans upside down. Some scholars believe that he was executed by Nero just after the Great Fire of Rome. The Romans blamed Christians for the tragedy. So, tradition has it, St. Peter's Basilica is built atop the very spot Peter was crucified.

Peter, the Rock.

In today's Gospel lection the resurrected Christ meets his disciples on the beach. They have been fishing. All night. Jesus had told them that they would fish together, only they would not fish for fish; they would fish for people. But Jesus is now dead. And the disciples' nets are empty.

On the beach this morning, even before they recognize him, Jesus tells them what to do. They do as instructed. Their nets grow full.

Everyone understands the first part of this story. If the disciples are to fish for people, they cannot do it without Jesus. And they do not have to worry. Jesus will be with them. Jesus will help them. It is going to be all right. With Jesus, because of Jesus, through the power of the resurrected Christ, they will be able to do what God has called them to do. Thank goodness. Thank God.

This is the gist of this first text from John. It is so hopeful. What a relief, that the frightened, lost, disillusioned disciples will be successful in their discipleship after all. God will see to it – through the resurrected Jesus. That is the first part.

The second pericope is painful, though. Gut-wrenchingly painful. At least it starts out that way.

Their nets are full. The disciples set their feet on shore. Jesus has started a charcoal fire. He says, "Come. Have breakfast." They are having communion. Jesus feeds them.

Here is the painful part: "Peter, do you love me?" Jesus asks Peter.

Has anyone asked you that question? Do you love me?

Sometimes we ask that question because we need to hear the answer. We need reassurance. We need to know that we are loved. Other times we ask that question because the other person needs to think things through. Why does Jesus ask Peter? "Peter, do you love me?"

The answer to Jesus' motives lays burning in that charcoal fire. It is not just any fire they are gathered around. Details matter. Jesus stands next to a charcoal fire.

If you go to Jerusalem today, there, at the southern tip of the old city, are ruins that archaeologists are near certain is Caiaphas' palace. Caiaphas was the High Priest. Before Caiaphas and the Sanhedrin handed Jesus to the Romans for execution, they examined Jesus, in this palace. Then, in the dark, they threw Jesus into the dungeon.

Amidst the palace ruins is a contemporary sculpture. It includes a Roman soldier. There are women there, too. And Peter. Peter is there, in bronze. And a rooster. Atop a Roman column, a rooster crows.

Is the story coming to mind? This is the scene of Peter's denial of Jesus. It is the last time in the biblical story that we have seen a charcoal fire. The Romans stand around a charcoal fire, warming themselves, and Peter hides in the distance. But the light, the light from the charcoal fire strikes Peter's face. They recognize him.

"You. Over there. Are not you a disciple of Jesus?"

Three times they ask Peter. Three times he denies his discipleship. As Jesus predicted he would. Around a charcoal fire.

And now, on the other side of crucifixion, after the empty tome, here they are, around a charcoal fire, with the resurrected Jesus. He feeds them, and he asks Peter, "Do you love me?"

Three times, the Romans ask Peter if he is Jesus' disciple, round aa charcoal fire. Three times, Jesus asks Peter, "Do you love me?" around a charcoal fire.

Baseball season started this week. For many people, Spring officially begins with the first pitch. Even if you are not a baseball fan you are surrounded by baseball terms. Baseball jargon and phrases have crept into our culture's aphorisms.

If someone "bats a thousand," they perform perfectly. If someone is a "heavy hitter," she is a person of influence, a very important person. If "you are in the big leagues," you have made it to the top of your profession. You can "take a rain check," or "knock it out of the park," or "swing for the fences," or you can "grandstand," and in every case the term comes from baseball. Baseball analogies sprinkle our cultural lexicon.

And you can "strike out." You can waste your first two chances and then, given one last opportunity, well, you can waste that one, too. Who hasn't? Who hasn't taken opportunity after opportunity, swing after swing, in some important effort, and then, in one final failing attempt, mussed that one up, too?

Maybe that is why Peter is hurt. Three times Peter had a chance to admit his love for Jesus, to confess publicly his discipleship, and three times Peter denied Jesus. Now, Jesus meets him by a charcoal fire and asks him three times, "Peter, do you love me?" Three times.

You know the baseball adage. Three times and you are out. Mess up the third time, and back to the benches. The phrase is so commonly used that in the 1990s, when lawmakers wanted to get tough on crime, they passed laws which mandate that if a person is charged with a third crime, the sentencing judge has no other option. No choice. No judicial alternative. Three times and you are out. Off to prison. Now, as you know, with penitentiaries bursting at the gates and with no discernable improvement in public safety or crime rates, lawmakers are reconsidering such draconian laws.

Jesus reconsidered them two millennia ago. On a beach. While feeding his disciples fish and bread. By a charcoal fire.

Peter, do you love me? Three strikes and you are … *in.*

What appears first as a painful, accusatory conversation reminiscent of Peter's denial of Jesus is in the end a comforting fireside chat. It is a scene of reconciliation. Forgiveness. Redemption. Grace.

"If you love me, feed my sheep."

In other words, welcome back. It is going to be like it was before. You can come back to what we used to do, together. We are going to fish for people, together.

We do, each of us, have a role to play in the economy of God. That is a fancy way to say that each of us has a job to do in God's restoration of the world. This is our call. This is our vocation. When you promised your very self to God– your life, your breath, your fortune, your soul! – God promised you that you would never want for meaningful work. Your life of discipleship would be risky, and hard, but also exciting, meaningful.

God is much better at keeping promises than we are. You know how it goes. Life gets busy. Cluttered. Complicated. Maybe your religious life has by now dwindled. Maybe you have become a pew Christian – here on Sunday without much thought about it otherwise. Perhaps your life of discipleship has come to be a thing of appearances only, of bland ritual of blind obedience to the ways of the world. Maybe you feel like you have struck out.

Today – here – now – Jesus beckons all of us to the charcoal fire. This is a scene of forgiveness. Redemption. Grace. And since the question is less about what has happened yesterday, and more about servanthood tomorrow, how will it be tomorrow that you can feed Jesus' sheep? What can you do to tend Jesus' lambs?

No matter what we have done, little worry about what we have left undone, today, you are back at bat. Three strikes and we are in. Thanks be to God.

# Reconciliation When We Don't Deserve It

## Genesis 33.1-4

*I do not do a great deal of narrative preaching, but this sermon required a retelling of a sweeping sage. It ends, however, with the passage and a poignant pastoral nudge. Ancient Biblical stories often reach strikingly contemporary applications.*

You know the story of Isaac and Rebekah's boys, twins; Esau was born first, Jacob just after, clutching Esau's heel. Papa Isaac loved Esau, the hunter. Mama Rebekah loved Jacob. Since Esau is the older of the two, he inherits the family's birthright, but when they grow up, Jacob tricks Esau out of the birthright. You might think that such trickery would bring hard feelings, estrangement event. You would be right.

That story is told way back in Genesis 25, eight chapters ago. Today Jacob and Esau meet again.

You may feel like you stepped out of the theater for popcorn and now that you are back, you cannot figure out how the story got from where you left it to where you rejoined it. Indeed, a lot has happened.

Jacob is a tricky one, a manipulator. He is always working the angles. Not only does he cheat Esau out of his birthright; Jacob deceives his father Isaac into giving him Isaac's one and only blessing. With Rebekah's help and complicity, Jacob puts on Esau's clothing and visits Isaac on his deathbed. He pretends to be Esau and old man Isaac, thinking he is blessing his eldest son before he dies, blesses Jacob instead.

Esau is beyond furious and hatches a plot of his own, to kill his brother Jacob. Rebekah learns of the plot, however, and warns Jacob, her favorite son, to run. She sends him far away to live with her brother Laban. So Jacob, having snookered Esau out of his birthright – Jacob, having deceived his father to steal Esau's blessing – must run away, far away. And he does.

Years pass. Jacob marries Rachel, his uncle's daughter, after fourteen years of waiting (but you know that story). At long last they have children, but not through Rachel. Rachel is not able to conceive so she – you guessed it – "gives" Jacob her handmaidens, who conceive, and give them children. By the time Rachel's sister Leah, and also Jacob's wife, contributes, Jacob has not one child but six, all of them boys.

Finally, Rachel conceives. They welcome yet another child, a boy, a son, named Joseph. With his growing family Jacob works hard, and it is not that long – 20 years – before he becomes prosperous. He becomes so prosperous that his wealth overshadows his uncle's wealth. There is grumbling in the family. God intervenes. "Go home," God says.

So Jacob and Rachel gather their wealth – animals, servants, and their family – and they flee in the night.

This is when things get really interesting.

After these long years, walking those miles home, Jacob must contemplate the turn his life is taking. Having plotted and deceived to obtain his brother's birthright and his father's blessing, he wonders how to make his way back into the family. Will his brother Esau receive him? Or, will their reunion simply awaken old animosities and stoke the fires of hatred and murder?

Jacob decides to send a peace offering. He chooses messengers to scout ahead. Find Esau, Jacob says. Tell him this: "I have lived with Laban as an alien, and stayed until now; and I have oxen, donkeys, flocks, male and female slaves; and I have sent to tell my lord, in order that I may find favor in your sight." '

Do you see what's happening? Perhaps Jacob is willing to apologize, but if an apology is not enough, he is prepared to pay. The messengers sprint ahead and do as they are instructed. Then, they return to Jacob. "We found Esau," they say. "He is coming to meet you," they say. "He is bringing 400 men with him," they say.

Well, Jacob assumes that he is in serious trouble now. He divides his people into two groups, splitting them, each taking livestock and provision. If Esau finds one group, Jacob thinks, and slaughters it, at least the other half will live. What is more, Jacob is still plotting, planning. He takes "two hundred female goats and twenty male goats, two hundred ewes and twenty rams, thirty camels and their colts, forty cows and ten bulls, twenty female donkeys and ten male donkeys." He places all of this livestock, this wealth, into the hands of his servants. And, he divides them up into subgroups. Jacob says to his servants, "Go ahead of me. Keep some distance between you. And," Jacob says, "when you come to Esau, here is what to say; this livestock belongs to your servant Jacob. They are a present. He is coming behind us."

Oh my oh my, is Jacob good. His plan is brilliant. Each group, three of them, will come upon Esau. Each time, Esau will receive a glorious gift, and surely, Jacob thinks, by the time the third livestock wave washes over Esau, he will relent and forgive. Great plan, eh? Jacob does all of this hoping to appease his angry brother Esau.

Then, Jacob goes to bed.

What happens next is as central to the story of Israel as almost any. You have heard the old saying that those with a clean conscience sleep well at night. Well, Jacob does not sleep well at all. He tosses and turns all night, and not by himself. He is visited by "a man." The man is not identified. He is just "a man." Jacob and the "man" wrestle until daybreak.

The storyteller wants us wondering who it is wrestling with Jacob. Is it Esau? Does Jacob wrestle with his conscience? Or, is Jacob wrestling with God? We do not know, we are not supposed to know, we cannot know. We know only that Jacob wrestles him to a draw. At dawn the "man" leaves, but not before giving Jacob a blessing.

Oh, and one more thing. Jacob finally tells us that his wrestling partner has been none other than God.

Oh, and yet one more thing; God changes Jacob's name. Now, Jacob will be called Israel. In a divine foreshadowing of the next chapter in God's story with God's people, Israel becomes the entry point for what God will do next.

And finally – you knew it was coming – there is yet one more thing. Jacob has been injured in the wrestling. It is his hip. He limps. He has a new name and a fresh blessing from God, but Jacob is not unscathed by the encounter. From now on, every step he takes will bring a flashback, a reminder that surely as God will use him to bring what is next, he must also recall the night he wrestled with conscience over all the deceit and trickery and dishonesty which had brought him to that point.

Now, finally, we are ready for the first four verses of Genesis, Chapter 33.

Can you see it? Can you imagine? Jacob looks up. He sees Esau. It is the first time in years. Esau comes towards Jacob, closing the distance, fast. And he is not alone. There are four hundred men with him. Jacob thinks quickly. He has already sent his servants ahead. At his side is his family, close family. He divides the children into groups. Leah takes some. Rachel takes some. Two maids command the remainder. The women and children go first. Does Jacob intend on using his own children as human shields? Is he hoping that seeing their shared bloodline will soften Esau's heart? Jacob shuffles them off, the maids first. Then Leah. Finally, Rachel escorts Joseph, their son, Israel's future. Having lined them up in the order of their importance – imagine how that must have felt! – then and only then does Jacob go to the front of the line.

Esau is closer now, closer and closer. Jacob bows, a sign of respect and contrition. He kneels not once but seven times. Esau keeps coming. Esau is running now. Esau is running toward Jacob. Closer and closer he comes until …

Esau arrives. He throws his arms around his brother Jacob, and Esau kisses Jacob, and they weep.

It is, I think, the most powerful scene of reconciliation in all of scripture. It is most powerful, it seems to me, because Jacob is the offender. Jacob does not deserve to be reconciled with Esau, not by human logic, not by earthly standards. Jacob has wronged his brother Esau. Jacob has every reason to expect Esau's wrath and retribution. By human standards of offense and vengeance, Esau might well draw his blade and cut his way back into birthright and blessing.

But he does not. Jacob and Esau kiss. They weep. They are brothers.

None of us reach adulthood without at least some discord, without at least a few scars. People hurt us, offend us, and, well, we offend others. If you are like most, and like me, you offend at least as frequently as you are offended.

I have deep respect for Alcoholics Anonymous and for its 12-step program. Many people work the 12 steps whether or not they battle addiction. The 12 steps are enormously useful for anyone wishing to deepen their spiritual lives.

Step 8 is instructive. It requires admitting that we have offended others. In fact, it asks us to catalogue the offenses. It reads: "Make a list of all persons we have harmed and become willing to make amends to them all." If you think Step 8 is demanding, wait until we get to Step 9: "Make direct amends to such people wherever possible, except when to do so would injure them or others."

Sometimes, reconciliation is possible only when the offender reaches out to the offended.

But sometimes, we are the offender. The good Gospel news is that reconciliation is actually possible. In fact, the entire Christian Gospel is about reconciliation, about reconciliation, aimed at reconciliation. The entire life and work of Jesus – birth, life, death, and resurrection – are about God's hope that we be reconciled, reconciled to God, reconciled to one another, reconciled to our deepest and best selves. The two are connected, you know. God reconciles us with God through Jesus Christ, and in this reconciliation, we discover the path to reconciliation with other people.

1 John announces that loving God and loving our brothers, loving our sisters, are one and the same. It is very blunt, in fact. "Those who say, 'I love God', and hate their brothers or sisters, are liars."

If we have offended others, if our offense divides us from others, God may well be nudging us towards confession and confrontation with those we have hurt. Remember that Jacob headed home to Esau because God commanded him to go.

Think of your life, of your relationships, of your past. Think of Jacob, crossing the distance, contrite and prepared.

Are there relationships in your life begging for a reconciliation that only your confession can begin?

# URACOG
## Deuteronomy 30.1-6 and Galatians 3.23-4.7

*Interpreting the sacraments is among the preacher's highest but most difficult tasks. In this sermon I wrestle with the practical implications of living into our baptismal identities.*

I no longer tell seatmates on airplanes that I am a minister. When I did, one of two things happened.

First, some wanted a counseling session, a request I would be happy to entertain in my office, but not within earshot of our stunned seatmates. Second, others wanted to argue about Christianity. They wanted to vent about their bad church experiences, or talk me out of my religious faith, or both.

Years ago, I revealed my reverend-ness to a seatmate who went ballistic in seat B. "Christianity is hogwash," he said. "The resurrection is fantasy, delusional retrojection," he went on. "Churches are full of judgmental, critical, and hypocritical people," he carried on, and on.

Finally, I interrupted. "You have to stop." I said. "You are talking about my people. I live and breathe and eat, church. I spend all my time with church people. They are my friends, my social network, and my employers. I know all about the church, and its failures, know all about its inconsistencies and its hypocrisies. And let me tell you, it is much worse than you think."

It is so good to be with my people on this Sunday morning!

We are a people, you and I. We are connected – bound, even – and bound not merely by shared commitments. Shared commitments are things we do. We are not connected most basically by things we do. We are connected by who we are. We are connected by something deeper still, older still, something beneath and below both our intellects and our wills.

We are connected by baptism. We are connected by God. There is but one connection that identifies and binds so profoundly that all rival identities fade away, all idolatrous commitments, all competing ideologies wilt and wither and die. Or at least they should. That identity is the one sealed within the waters of baptism.

The first infant I baptized, I buried to brain cancer seven years later. She would be in her mid-twenties now. I know in my spiritual bones that we remain connected, she and I. And I remain connected to her parents. These ties are more than <u>memory</u>, more than <u>emotion</u>, more than <u>affection</u>. We remain connected in Jesus Christ and our baptism in his name, that is if we still believe that the sacrament is sacramental, that is.

It is worth remembering that even the word sacrament is hard to get our heads around. Our word sacrament comes from a Middle English word; before that, it was Old French. Before that, it was Latin, meaning "solemn oath," from a word meaning "to hallow" or "sacred." Before that, it was Greek, from a word meaning "mystery." When we say the word sacrament, we pronounce a word filtered across more than two millennia through four languages, and it *began* as a mystery.

So when we read the nice, neat, numbered explanations of baptism in the *Book of Order* it is helpful to remember that what began in mystery can be somewhat difficult to nail down on newsprint. Which is to say that sometimes, faith is involved, which leads us to Galatians 3. There is likely not a preacher here who has not waxed rhapsodic on Galatians 3 and 4. You know the theo-logic.

Before, there was law. It was a disciplinarian. Then, before Jesus, God's people were something like minors named in a will. Someday, we would inherit the estate. Until then, however, God's people were slaves.

This tension between slavery and freedom is paradigmatic in the Hebrew scriptures. That is why we read from Deuteronomy. This text was clearly written to exiles.

My mother was a high school honors English teacher. It is a traumatic thing, being raised with a dictionary at the dinner table. Mom taught us that prepositions matter. Think about Deuteronomy's prepositions. If you call to mind the blessings and curses I have set before you, if you are exiled to the ends of the earth, then the Lord will have compassion on you, and circumcise your heart, and you will love the Lord your God. For those who want to label and libel the Old Testament God as a God only of wrath and judgement, take note. It is more complex than that.

What might seem qualified in the Old Testament becomes clear and unqualified in the New. Look at Galatian's prepositions. (My mother would be so proud.)

If you belong to Christ, if a child, then also an heir, through God.

How is it that we come to belong to Christ? Baptism. Belonging is not, then, something that *we* do. Belonging is not, then, something that we *do*. Belonging is something that we *are* because of what God *does*.

Walter Brueggemann poses this single, profound observation. "Ideology," Brueggemann observes, "is trying to talk us out of our baptismal identity." That identity? Children of God. We are children of God. What Walter Brueggemann calls ideology might be precisely what the Apostle Paul calls "the elemental spirits of the world," as in "we were enslaved to the elemental spirits of the world."

In many ways, the elemental spirits, the ideologies luring us away from our baptisms, have not changed all that much. Paul mentions baptism's power to unite us beyond Jew and Greek. Ethnic and racial identities continue to lure us out of our baptismal unity. Listen to the subtext of every conversation regarding immigration policy. Consider that people are still protesting in Ferguson, Missouri, a year after the racially charged civil unrest there. Charleston will spend decades healing after the racist murder of nine Christians gathered to study the Bible. I do not need to tell you about racism's deep wounds and intractable allure.

Is it possible that our baptismal identities can overwhelm even racism and ethnic prejudice?

Paul mentions also baptism's power to unite us beyond male and female. Gender continues to be a dividing wall in our world. Women's suffrage in our nation is not a century old yet. Women's ordination in our tradition is younger still. Today? Equal pay? Glass ceilings? Is it possible that our baptismal identities can overwhelm even sexism?

Paul mentions also baptism's power to unite us beyond slave and free. He spoke of literal slavery, of course, but Hebrew scripture teaches that slavery and freedom are paradigmatic, metaphorical.

As for me, I am convinced that all divisions – ethnic, racial, and gender – are ultimately expressed and perpetuated in economic freedom and in economic slavery. And nothing seems more enslaving, therefore, than the temptation to base our identities in producing and consuming, in buying and selling, in having and holding. Believing so makes one neither anti-capitalist or anti-business. Anything but. We wish only to observe the idolatrous effort of modern capitalism to redefine the purpose of humanity. Our economic system, in its unchecked extremes, is willing to posit a redefinition of our identity. It dares propose a new explanation of humanity's purpose. In its unexamined proposal, people are worth the houses we inhabit, the salaries we draw, the cars we drive, the clothes we wear, the resources we command. One's worth is thought to be *material* – hence, *material*ism. Net worth is the term we use. Our net worth is the sum total of what we own. Are we to be identified by what we own?

Christians know that one's worth is not determined by the cut of our clothing, the gloss of our cars, or the complexity of our 1040s. We know that we are worthy because we have been claimed by Jesus Christ in our baptisms. We are children of God.

To the ideologies of the age which tempt us to forget or to deny our baptismal identities, we are emboldened to step toe-to-toe and to declare with a loud and bold voice, we are not slaves to your diminished and utilitarian definition of our worth! We are children of God, sealed by the Holy Spirit and marked as Christ's forever. Nothing anyone ever says or does can make that not true.

Why did God command Abraham to sacrifice Isaac when Isaac was twelve? Because if God had waited until Isaac was thirteen, it would not have been a sacrifice.

My thirteen-year-old son does not like this joke. Neither did his older sisters. By the time they hit thirteen, they had heard this joke many times. But they had heard this far more often. "You are a child of God, sealed by the Holy Spirit, and marked as Christ's forever. Nothing anyone ever says or does can make that no true." When they were children, I tried to repeat this litany to them every single day. I would trace the sign of the cross on their foreheads and repeat the litany – they would say that I repeated it ad nauseum. One of my children, then about seven, looked up at me one day as I started the litany. "You are a child of God," I began.

"I know, I know," she interrupted, rolling her eyes, and then the continued, "sealed by the Holy Spirit. Nothing anyone says or does can make that no true." She was being sarcastic, but she knew the litany, the entire litany, all of it.

This liturgy describes our baptismal identity. I said it hoping to provide an alternative to the competing messages they received about who they are and why they matter. Like all teenagers, these rival identities no doubt poked at them and prodded, in the classroom, on the ballpark, in the back seat, and at the shopping mall. When these rival identities were singing their siren songs, I wanted my children to lapse almost involuntarily into this mantra, "You are a child of God, sealed by the Holy Spirit, marked as Christ's forever. Nothing anyone ever says or does can make that not true."

That is why every baptism I have officiated for two decades has included these words. Just after baptizing in the name of the Father and of the Son and of the Holy Ghost I make the sign of the cross on the infant's head and I say those words. Child. God. Sealed. Marked. Forever.

That is why every congregation I have served has asked the parents of those presented for baptism to do the same things. Every day. Sign of the cross. Litany. Child. God. Sealed. Marked. Forever.

That is the message because that is our identity. That is our baptismal identity. We are God's children, included in God's family. No matter what elemental spirits try to lure and lull us into another understanding, that is who we are.

Which is the other aspect of our baptismal identity, of course. If I am a child of God, then I am to grow to learn that baptism is not only about me and my identity. It is about you, too, and about being included in community, Christ's body, and about what it means to be engaged in God's corporate call to participate in God's ongoing redemption and restoration of the world. I am God's child. You are God's child. Together we are God's family. This means specific things in the world, to which we turn out gaze in the morning.

Two of my kids have now flown the coup. They are off into God's world, learning and experimenting and failing and succeeding and all of it, I pray, rooted in their baptismal identities. When they left home and I was no longer able to make the sign of the cross on their foreheads, or in the air across the room, and start the litany, since those days were over, I defaulted to technology. I resorted to texting.

Texting requires brevity, of course, so that litany – you are a child of God, etc. – got shortened. Then and now, before I go to bed, I text them this. URACOG. You are a child of God. URACOG. Each night, in their dorm rooms, their phones would announce a text from Dad. URACOG.

They began responding as you would think. "I love you," they might text. "Goodnight, Dad," they sometimes responded.

Then, one night my oldest texted back in a way that revealed something new, something profound. She was figuring out it.

URACOG, I reminded her.

Her texted response was brief. She texted, "You, too."

145

CPSIA information can be obtained
at www.ICGtesting.com
Printed in the USA
FFHW020257301118
49684997-54077FF